FRUITFUL EMBRACES

Also by Evelyn and James Whitehead

Christian Life Patterns
A Sense of Sexuality
Shadows of the Heart
Wisdom of the Body
Transforming Our Painful Emotions
Holy Eros
Nourishing the Spirit

FRUITFUL EMBRACES

Sexuality, Love, and Justice

EVELYN EATON WHITEHEAD
and JAMES D. WHITEHEAD

TRUE DIRECTIONS
AN AFFILIATE OF TARCHER BOOKS

iUniverse®

FRUITFUL EMBRACES
SEXUALITY, LOVE, AND JUSTICE

New Revised Standard Version Bible: Catholic Edition, copyright 1989, 1993, Division of Christian Education of the National Council of the Churches of Christ in the United States of America. Used by permission. All rights reserved.

iUniverse books may be ordered through booksellers or by contacting:

iUniverse
1663 Liberty Drive
Bloomington, IN 47403
www.iuniverse.com
1-800-Authors (1-800-288-4677)

ISBN: 978-1-4917-4414-7 (sc)
ISBN: 978-1-4917-4415-4 (hc)
ISBN: 978-1-4917-4413-0 (e)

Library of Congress Control Number: 2014914249

Printed in the United States of America.

iUniverse rev. date: 9/9/2014

Contents

Introduction

As cradle Catholics, both of us came of age during the exciting years of the Second Vatican Council in the early 1960s. Newly married when we began our joint teaching career at Loyola University Chicago in 1970, we were largely unaware of the rich complexity of human sexuality and gender. This naiveté would be transformed by the wisdom and courage of those who participated in our university courses over the subsequent forty-five years.

During the 1970s, these colleagues—educators, pastors, chaplains, religious sisters, lay leaders—affirmed the positive role of crises in their lives. From these fertile discussions, our first book emerged: *Christian Life Patterns: The Psychological Challenges and Invitations of Adult Life* (1979). In the 1980s, the pastoral focus shifted to explorations of the links between sexuality and Christian spirituality. The vital connections here are clear, since both of these dynamics embody the desire for life in abundance. But often they are cast in opposition. Two books emerged from these discussions: *A Sense of Sexuality: Christian Love and Intimacy* (1990) and *Wisdom of the Body: Making Sense of Our Sexuality* (2001).

Those who joined our course discussion in the 1990s were often eager to examine the role of emotions in adult life and Christian spirituality. Of particular concern were the volatile dynamics of anger, guilt, fear, and shame. These productive explorations generated two books: *Shadows of the Heart: A Spirituality of the Negative Emotions* (1994) and *Transforming Our Painful Emotions* (2010).

The new century's arrival focused our attention on the image of Eros, the energy that animates our emotions and focuses our desires. We explore these concerns in *Holy Eros: Pathways to a Passionate God*

(2009) and *Nourishing the Spirit: The Healing Emotions of Wonder, Joy, Compassion, and Hope* (2012).

In recent years, the faculty and ministry participants at the Institute of Pastoral Studies at Loyola have brought issues of justice—in both Christian life and the broader social arena—into greater focus. This shared commitment has drawn us to fuller consideration of the themes we examine in this present volume: *Fruitful Embraces: Sexuality, Love, and Justice.*

In part 1, our reflection begins in exploring the dynamics of sensuality, intimacy, vulnerability, and self-care that energize our vital relationships. In part 2, we give explicit consideration to the links between sexuality and justice: honoring the disabled body, acknowledging the clergy sexual abuse in the Catholic Church, and tracing the emerging social commitment to marriage equality. We conclude this section with a broader reflection on an enduring tension evident in the Christian tradition's theology of sexuality: the pessimism of Augustine in the West and the optimism of Gregory of Nyssa in the East.

In part 3, we explore the Christian embrace of compassion and the ways that this core value comes into play in an understanding of sexual diversity. Three subsequent chapters examine the psychological and spiritual experiences of transgender persons—a new and often bewildering consideration for many of us as Christians. The final chapter offers a reflection on a prophetic Christian ministry in support of sexuality and justice.

As we explore the complex questions of sexuality and gender diversity, we acknowledge the wisdom and support we have received from Sister Luisa Derouen, OP, and Sister Clarice Sevegney, OP. It is to these experienced pastoral mentors that we dedicate this book.

PART ONE
Relationships

Chapter One

In the Beginning: Christian Sensuality

> *A woman came to him with an alabaster jar of very costly*
> *ointment, and she poured it on his head as he sat at the*
> *table.* —Matthew 26:6

The Sensual Surround of Infancy

We are launched at birth into myriad embraces. The newborn baby survives by being held and warmed, cleaned, and coddled. Doting parents caress the infant with delight and affection. Grandparents, siblings, and nannies multiply the touches that enfold the growing child. As children, we are blessed with this intimate contact, soothed in ways that confirm our safety and belonging. Good touch signals that we are not alone, and this connection strengthens self-confidence. Nourishing touch is the foundation of secure attachment, through which the child comes to appreciate that the world is trustworthy. This early confidence, born of nurturing touch, introduces the child to the virtues of hope and trust that will guide him or her over a lifetime.

In her evocative book *Erotic Attunement*, moral theologian Christina Traina reflects on the sensual connections between mother and infant. These intimate exchanges reveal the essential dynamics of sensuality, long before the later movements of sexual development and genital behavior. Traina recalls the ecstasy and exhaustion of these initial embraces. "What emotions, sensations, associations, body memories, and images accompany the physical care of small children? What is the quality of the

1

experience of exhaustedly, helplessly nestling a finally sleeping newborn in the crook of one's neck, rocking by a window at dawn? Of nursing a too-hungry infant at a too-full breast after a stressful day?" She concludes, "These may not be moments of pure selflessness, or of sexual arousal, but they are benevolent and they are erotic." *Benevolent* and *erotic*: a healthy starting point for a Christian spirituality of sensuality.

These nurturing exchanges in the first months of life provide privileged insight into the essential role of sensuality throughout our life. This early season teaches two essential lessons upon which our experience of mature sexuality and committed love will depend: dependency on others need not diminish us and vulnerability is part of our charm.

Christian Sensuality

"Sensuality is open, self-conscious enjoyment of the senses' pleasures, an enjoyment that includes hunger but also satiation, indulgence but also restraint and even selective abstinence, and most of all, patient anticipation and savoring." For Traina, sensuality incorporates the awareness of bodily sensations and taking pleasure in these sensations in order to be more fully present in our bodies. Through this sensual experience, we are reminded that our experience of grace arises only in and through the body. The body bears sacramental significance.

Christians today are returning to a richer appreciation of the goodness of creation: how the sights and sounds, the tastes and touches that give shape to our world are gifts of God—thrilling attunements to creation, even if these delights may sometimes be distorted. A religious faith founded in a belief in "the Word made flesh" should be good news for the body and all its sensuous possibilities. The deep suspicion of sensuality, characteristic of the Western church's influential theologian Augustine, now commands less and less authority. The experience of many Christians today affirms the insight of the great theologian of the Eastern church, Gregory of Nyssa. Gregory appreciated the role of earthly delights in directing our attention toward the Creator. For many contemporary Christians, the spiritual journey includes a wholehearted embrace of personal embodiment, expressed in the sensual bonds that unite us with others in justice and love.

Christian faith encourages us to honor God's presence through our senses. We care for our own bodies; we reach out to other bodies with affection and respect; we welcome the sensual pleasures of food and drink and sexual delight; and we take time to savor beauty. But life does not always unfold in such a fortunate way. As Americans, for example, we inhabit a climate of addiction. An epidemic of obesity, matched by the prevalence of anorexia, undermines our appreciation of food. Widespread alcoholism raises alarm; the sexual abuse of children by clergy and other authority figures leaves us suspicious of affectionate touch; and pornography celebrates bodies disengaged from genuine contact.

Yet throughout history and continuing today, Christians have honored the healthy stirrings of sensuality as essential to human flourishing. But along with this continuing commitment, Christian spirituality acknowledges that enjoyment of these essential goods is not humanity's final goal. Thus many on the spiritual journey choose to fast—for a time—from the ordinary enjoyment of food and drink and touch. This abstinence is chosen not as self-punishment but as witness to a deeper truth, in Traina's words:

> Bodily goods are not ultimate goods. Our good in God
> transcends a good meal, a comforting hug, warm clothes,
> and all those other physical things that we both need
> and enjoy. This care to protect, delight in, and celebrate
> the body without idolizing its goods is one of the keys to
> Christian ethics of sexuality.

The first Christians gathered in communal meals to remember and celebrate that final meal that Jesus had taken with his friends. Here the repeated pleasure of bread and wine, shared among the gathered body of believers, created a liturgy both sensual and sacred. This intuition would become a cornerstone of Catholic belief: sensual experiences of eating and anointing, the liturgical delights of color and incense—these may bring believers closer to the mysterious presence of God. Sensuous pleasure, itself a gift of creation, can open us to God's sacred and saving presence. So it is that sacramental rituals serve as central acts of faith. Traina expresses this deeply Catholic conviction:

> We wash, and we are baptized; we eat, and we partake of
> Eucharist; we touch to heal, transfer power, and comfort,

and we absolve, confirm, ordain, anoint the sick. In each
of these six sacraments the body is sign and symbol of a
sacred reality, a mystery. Our tradition teaches that in
marriage the union of bodies is also a sign and symbol
of grace that is really present.

This audacious belief, with its dazzling optimism about the sensual
experience of faith, became in the course of Christian history difficult to
sustain. Doubt about the healthy companionship of the sensual and the
sacred was registered in the Catholic Church's judgments that priestly
leaders should not marry. The service of leadership, so closely linked with
the sacred liturgy, seemed to demand a distance from sexuality. Later,
the hearty bread prepared in family hearths for sharing at the Eucharist
was replaced by thin white wafers prepared in institutional ovens. Now
distanced from everyday bread, this sacred wafer was understood to
better represent the "bread of angels" (*panis angelicus*). In the Protestant
Reformation of the sixteenth century, reformers distanced their worship
from its traditional sensual accompaniments—the candles and incense
and colorful vestments that had been part of the earlier liturgical
tradition. Proscriptions against dance and alcohol, characteristic of
many evangelical Christian communities, gave further evidence of what
philosopher Charles Taylor has described as an *excarnation* of Christian
faith—"the transfer of our religious life out of bodily forms of ritual,
worship, practice, so that it comes more and more to reside in the head."
This shift moved faith away from its incarnational roots. "Christianity,
as the faith of the Incarnate God, is denying something essential to itself
as long as it remains wedded to forms which *excarnate*."

As Christians lost confidence in the sensual as an avenue to grace,
they came to see the beautiful and the pleasurable in life as temptations
distracting from their efforts to embrace religious faith. Influenced by
Augustine's pessimism, they understood human nature itself as corrupt,
incapable of embracing the sensual without sin. In the following pages we
will draw frequently on the Christian spirituality of sensuality advanced
by moral theologian Christina Traina. Throughout her discussion, Traina
reminds us that sensual pleasures—a warm bath, a stunning sunset, an
inspiring musical selection—can be erotic without being sexual in the
sense of genital stimulation. Our sensual responsiveness occurs along a

broad continuum, and in many instances, the urgent and genital quality of sexuality is absent from sensuality.

The Healing Marvel of Touch

If some touch is forbidden, is other touch required?
—Traina

Physical touch is the first language of the human species. And throughout our lives, touch continues as a profound vehicle of personal expression and communication. Our touch communicates a wide range of feelings: compassion and sympathy, fear and anger, trust and domination, affection and joy. When we are fortunate, good touch comes to us first within the family. Later we learn the affectionate gestures of friendship—a welcoming handshake, a friendly hug, a reassuring pat on the back. With our lover we explore the nuances of sexual touch, in romantic caress and passionate embrace.

Neuroscientists have identified the biological responses triggered by good touch. Touching the sensitive neurons in the skin sends signals to the reward areas of the brain, diminishing the levels of cortisol in the bloodstream. This reduction of physiological stress promotes trust and cooperation. Good touches benefit both the giver and the receiver: the person who initiates affectionate touch—and the fortunate recipient— experience these physiological effects. Good touch communicates well-being, care, reassurance. Physical contact that is violent or coercive generates fear, leading us to withdraw from other people.

Of all the senses, touch is the most powerful in the healing of wounds. Before the widespread development of medical technology, physicians would characteristically place an ear on the patient's chest or back to listen for heartbeat and lung activity. The prevalence today of the stethoscope and other diagnostic equipment makes this simple gesture of caring touch and concern obsolete. Critics warn that these technological advances risk eliminating physicians' most effective practice—touching the patient. Even so, many health care professionals—physicians, nurses, physical therapists— continue to appreciate touch as crucial in diagnostic exams and follow-up procedures. Beyond the medical examination room, too, hands have the ability to read the environment. Many who have lost the power of sight use their hands effectively to explore their surroundings. Sighted people, too, use hands to examine objects more closely and to hold a treasured object safe.

Psychological research records the healing effects of touch for both body and psyche. And more and more evidence arises recognizing the human hand—what Dacher Keltner calls "the five-digit wonder"— as a potent source of restorative energy. The American Psychological Association reports that, prior to the pharmaceutical revolution of the early 1940s, touching, massaging, and rubbing the body were the major therapeutic interventions offered by physicians. Today, strong empirical support, reinforced by personal testimony, identifies massage therapy as successful in diminishing depression and enhancing the immune system. And renewed interest in practices of healing touch has expanded the availability of touch therapy in both critical care settings and health maintenance programs. The pioneering empirical research of Tiffany Fields at the Touch Research Institute initially focused on the role of touch in human infants born prematurely. Now the scope has expanded in five worldwide locations conducting therapeutic programs and scientific research. The findings from these international studies confirm the ways in which touch supports health throughout the life span.

Despite this evidence, healthy nurturing touch is not available to many adults in the United States. In US cultural settings, a close adult relationship beyond one's immediate family is frequently understood to imply romantic attachments or sexual intent. This cultural convention narrows the availability of adult touch. For their part, many US adults enjoy healthy touch in interacting with household pets, whose presence provides opportunities for physical contact and play. Health clubs offer massage sessions; both women and men schedule appointments with hair stylists and manicurists, whose services include attentive nonsexual touch. But still, many Americans have difficulty meeting their own needs for nourishing touch.

Jesus and Touch

> *Someone touched me; for I noticed that power had gone out from me.* —Luke 8:46

Mindful of the importance of nourishing embraces, we recall the healing touches that marked Jesus's ministry. Jesus entered a house where his friend's mother-in-law lay in bed with a fever. Jesus "came and took her by the hand and lifted her up. Then the fever left her and she began to serve them" (Mark 1:31). In Matthew's Gospel, a leper—whose touch is to be, at all costs, avoided—kneels before Jesus, believing that Jesus can choose to heal him. Jesus "stretched out his hand and touched him, saying, 'I do choose; be made clean.' Immediately his leprosy was cleansed" (Matthew 8:2–3). Word of Jesus's powerful touch spread to many. "As the sun was setting, all those who had any who were sick with various kinds of diseases brought them to him; and he laid his hands on each of them and cured them" (Luke 4:40).

This healing touch was not always initiated by Jesus. In Luke's Gospel we read of an ill woman who dares to approach Jesus as he moves with his disciples through a crowded street. Suddenly he senses he has been touched in a special way. "Who touched me?" he asked. His disciples reminded him that they were pushing against many people as they moved through the crowd. But he insisted: "Someone touched me; for I noticed that power had gone out from me" (Luke 8:46). This woman's expectant touch released God's healing power—to Jesus's surprise. In a very different context, Jesus attended a banquet where he allowed himself to be touched by a woman of questionable reputation. Luke's Gospel gives a more elaborate and sensual account of this encounter than does Matthew's Gospel: "She stood behind him at his feet, weeping, and began to bathe his feet with her tears and to dry them with her hair. Then she continued kissing his feet and anointing them with the ointment" (Luke 7:38). Here the sensual touch of oil on skin marks an anointing of Jesus as he approaches his death.

Massage: A Sacrament of Touch

A friend writes of his experience of massage:

> As I climbed aboard the table I shed my towel, my last link to modesty. Swiftly I was swathed in several sheets. After briefly rubbing my upper arms and neck, the therapist began to ply my forearm, flexing my wrist and rubbing each finger. It was as if the creator was taking tactile inventory of my body. As I felt nerves come alive, I mused on the extraordinary invention that was my arm.

7

Turning me over, the therapist kneaded the backs of my thighs and calves. As his hands moved upwards, my lower back and hips murmured their gratitude. With steady, insistent but not too strong pressure, he greeted the dwellings of fatigue, anxiety and no doubt, many other emotions. As I lay resting on the table after the massage, I mused on the many graces of the massage. The hands of the therapist had shown a striking respect for my body. My hesitancy had given way to comfort and trust. After exchanging a few words, he fell silent. For thirty minutes I heard only the humming of tissues, nerves and muscles.

As his hands pressed and molded my flesh, I felt how strange and ordinary, how utterly rare and commonplace this touching was. This was as everyday as kneading dough or washing a small child. A humble gift to the body produced unnamed sensations from unknown nerves, trembles from grateful muscles. The experience was not sexual, but was intensely sensual. This privileged touching of flesh seemed exceptional, even exotic. But it was also most ordinary: this was simply skilled, graceful touch—attention to neglected flesh. I thought of my life and those of loved ones, deprived of this delight by busyness, modesty, woundedness. Had Christianity not veered so far from the flesh, massage might have become a sacrament (communication to authors).

A Christian Theology of Touch

It is as possible and as wrong to touch too little as too much.
—Traina

Thomas Aquinas, writing in the thirteenth century, limited his consideration of touch to sexual and genital contact within marriage. Traina observes that "the absence of the vast majority of pleasurable touch from his treatment is curious." She adds, "The possibility that physical affection might be as important as food is to individual flourishing, or as sex is to the human race, does not occur to Thomas." Thomas's narrow focus reduced the ethics of touch to the ethics of intercourse. He did not have Augustine's deep suspicion of touch, but he nevertheless seemed to assume that touch was not essential to our survival. Thus, all physical contact beyond sexual touch was not morally relevant.

A Christian theology of touch finds its home within the virtue of temperance, which means the balanced enjoyment of food, drink, and sex—all things that God has created for our good. The virtue of chastity, in turn, is rooted in the practice of temperance, but "in the tradition, chastity by definition is about intercourse, which in turn entails observing the absolute limits set by theology of marriage." For those who are not married, abstaining from sexual touch is an absolute; here there is no room for temperance with its balancing of "not too much, not too little."

The virtue of temperance is not abstinence but balance. "The temperate person avoids not only overeating and obsession with food, but also undernourishment and revulsion toward food. This suggests that a discussion of chastity would begin with touch, discuss the dangers of excessive and inadequate touch, and then treat intercourse as a special case" (Traina). Despite his disinterest in nonsexual touch, Thomas did recognize that the virtue of temperance is meant to balance sensual pleasure, and he believed that to reject the sensual pleasure we are meant to experience in creation is to offend the Creator. Anglican priest Jim Cotter writes, "to discern when and how to touch and be touched is an ascetical task: to live by the Spirit is neither not to touch, so hating the flesh, nor to touch indiscriminately, which takes no account of the needs of the other." Traina concludes, "the pleasure of affectionate touch may then not just be acceptable within a life of radical discipleship but essential to it."

Erotic Attunement: A Sensual Discipline

With the metaphor "erotic attunement," Traina brings together an ethic of sensuality that governs all the ways we link lives with others and an ethic of touch that measures the many vital ways we make contact with one another. For Traina, erotic attunement best expresses the goal of our enduring relations with one another, from child-rearing, to enduring friendships, to marriage. Erotic attunement is not limited to "sexy

9

connections" but is intended to include the many expressions of sensual bonding that unite us with our children, friends, and marriage partners.

Attunement suggests the rhythmic movement of partners. This aesthetic metaphor "combines perception, imagination, and experimentation in an endless, partnered dance." The dance answering the partner's needs and desire is the substance of the virtue. The image of dance raises the question: who leads? Attunement avoids domination (I must always lead) by honoring the shifting contribution of different partners in the movement. Erotic attunement, for Traina, points to the affectionate relationships we forge with others as we adjust our movements of approach and withdrawal, of intimacy and solitude.

In traditional moral theology, *right relation* was the term used to describe the proper arrangement between persons. This legal image is more static, emphasizing an established pattern of rights and duties. Attunement suggests a flexibility shaped by attentive presence and by a changing pace as we seek a rhythm that harmonizes our life and that of another. Attunement is a dynamic measure of the relationships we develop with each other.

Erotic attunement harmonizes our experience of duty and desire, measuring our desires in light of others' needs. Traina judges that "Sensual desire cannot be separated from questions of care and justice, for it is only through the senses, in the end, that I can relate to my neighbors or learn what justice to them requires." If our erotic sensibilities are out of tune, being attentive to other people's needs and respectful of their vulnerabilities is difficult. She concludes, "One way to evaluate my desires is to ask how they shape the ways I care for others and learn what those others need and deserve from me."

Erotic attunement supports sexual maturity. Paul Ricoeur describes the evolution of our erotic sensibility from a raw instinctual arousal to the sophisticated engagement of tenderness. Tenderness is "sexual energy released from the force of a blind drive; it is sexuality personalized." Tenderness—the fruit of erotic attunement—humanizes sexual energy, allowing love to find fulfillment in bonds of mutually satisfying and fruitful committed love. Tenderness serves as the portal through which the deep instinct of sexuality is humanized and our sexual desire is personalized. If our erotic energy is out of tune, we are more likely to succumb to the energy of lust. Ricoeur describes lust with the term eroticism—"a restless desire for pleasure" that is disengaged from any "lasting and intimate interpersonal bond." When tenderness is displaced by eroticism, "an egoistic cultivation of pleasure wins out over mutual exchange." Empathy and compassion are lost, and erotic attunement is defeated.

Traina concludes that an ethic of touch must finally become a cultivated habit and a virtue. For her, the traditional vocabulary of temperance and chastity seems too narrowly focused to be able to support the broader moral discussion needed today. In her own work, she has adopted the term erotic attunement. It is here that sensuality and justice come together. "If attunement is perceptive cultivation of right relation between persons, attunement is simply justice approached from the direction of intimacy."

Ethics and Aesthetics Embrace

> O taste and see that the LORD is good.
> —Psalm 34:8

In the earliest scriptural memory, beauty and goodness walked hand in hand. Surveying God's handiwork, the Creator repeatedly exclaims, "It is good. It is very good!" (Genesis 1:10, 12, 18, 21, 25, 31). In the biblical garden, woman and man walked naked and unashamed—both beautiful and good. But in the biblical account, something soon goes badly amiss. Catastrophe intervenes, and shame sweeps in. Bodies must now be hidden from one another, as our ancestors set about the sweaty toil of childbearing and breadwinning.

Christian commentators have attempted to provide explanations for this troubling state of affairs. Haunted by his own troubled history, Augustine determined that the force of this original transgression continues to affect humankind. Beauty now becomes suspect, beguiling humans and tempting us toward sinful behavior. The marvels of creation and the world's delights now stand in tension with our goal of eternal life. Here a chasm opens between the aesthetic and the ethical.

The triumph of reason in Western culture, funded by both the scientific revolution and the philosophical Enlightenment, sealed the schism. Ethics developed as a highly rational discipline, committed to a logical demonstration and rigorous proof of unchanging laws of conduct. In its search for justice, ethics had little time for beauty. Aesthetics, near neighbor of the emotions, came to be seen as an unreliable resource in the pursuit of truth and goodness.

Many thoughtful people today are weary of the barrier that separates the ethical from the aesthetic. Severed from its partner, each of these manifestations of the human spirit has suffered. In different fields of study, scholars are exploring ways to overcome this artificial schism. One effort begins in recognition of moral beauty. Theologian Sally McFague insists, "It is the aesthetic appreciation for the Other—God and our neighbors—that prompts the ethical response."

Beauty—in sight or sound or memory—demands our attention. Often we stop what we are doing so that we may be more aware of beauty before us. Alerted to the fragility of an antique vase or the delicate loveliness of a small child, we become more attentive, more respectful. Literary critic Elaine Scarry observes that it is this *arresting quality* of beauty that links aesthetics and ethics. "Noticing its beauty increases the possibility that it will be carefully handled."

Aesthetic appreciation both opens our hearts to righteous living and prompts compassion for those precious parts of life that require attentive care. As Sallie McFague insists, "[B]eauty and need, aesthetics and ethics, God and the world, join at the place where people praise God and serve the basic needs of others." At their best, both ethics and aesthetics lead to the respectful embraces where sexuality and justice unite.

Throughout this book, we will promote the embrace of the emotional and the rational, the sensual and the cognitive, and—most especially—the marriage of sexuality and justice.

Additional Resources

In this chapter we draw on three of Christina Traina's texts on the links between sensuality and Christian spirituality. See especially pages 65, 116, 184, 217, 241-3 in her *Erotic Attunement: Parenthood and the Ethics of Sensuality between Unequals*. See pages 73, 79, and 93 in her essay, "Under Pressure: Sexual Discipleship in the Real World," in *Sexuality and the U.S. Catholic Church*. And we also quote from her online essay, "Roman Catholic Resources for an Ethic of Sexuality." Paper delivered at the Common Ground Conference, March 5–7, 2004. Accessed at www. npic.org/commonground/papers/trainapaper.html.

Paul Ricoeur discusses the evolved capacity for tenderness in his essay, "Wonder, Eroticism and Enigma," in *Sexuality and the Sacred: Sources for Theological Reflection*. Charles Taylor's observation about *excarnation* appears in his *A Secular Age*.

Through her work at the Touch Research Institute at the University of Miami, Tiffany Fields has pioneered development of therapeutic responses based on the healing properties of touch; she reports these developments in *Touch* and in *Healing Heartbreak*. Dacher Keltner examines the psychological aspects of touch in his *Born to Be Good: The Science of a Meaningful Life*.

Jim Cotter includes touch in his discussion of "Homosexual and Holy," in *The Way*. Also see his consideration of respectful touch in *Pleasure, Pain and Passion*.

In *Transcendence and Beyond* Sallie McFague explores links between the aesthetic and the ethical; see especially the chapter "Intimations of Transcendence, Praise and Compassion." Elaine Scarry links beauty and care in *On Beauty and Being Just*.

Chapter Two

Loving Well: Attachment, Vulnerability, and Devotion

Where you go, I will go; where you lodge, I will lodge; your people shall be my people, and your God, my God.

—Ruth 1:16

The Bible gives an account of the fierce friendship that developed between two vulnerable women—Ruth, a recent widow, and Naomi, her aged mother-in-law. The story of their growing attachment and mutual devotion has inspired lovers and poets across the centuries. Their story focuses our attention here on the dynamics of loving well.

Love is not a single feeling but a complex set of emotions. These emotions embrace a wide range of relationships: early romance, parental devotion, the lifelong affection of spouses, the easy companionship among friends, a caregiver's commitment to a person in need, the warm feelings we have for those who have cared for us. Each of these expressions can rightly be identified as love. But these relationships differ from one another both in the emotional tone and in the behavior that flows from our feelings.

Many of the feelings associated with love—joy, contentment, sexual arousal, shared pleasure, gratitude—we appreciate as positive. But painful emotions, too, can arise in the context of love relationships: disappointment, jealousy, resentment, grief. And love encompasses more than our feelings. Love involves choice and commitment, moving us toward responses of generosity, forgiveness, care, and concern.

Exploring the Roots of Love

Psychologists are interested in how we mature as lovers, how we develop the personal resources required in our close relationships. For many authors today—social scientists and spiritual writers alike—attachment theory serves as a valuable resource as we attempt to understand these complex dynamics. Based on the pioneering work of British psychologist John Bowlby and his American colleague Mary Ainsworth, attachment theory suggests that effective nurturing in infancy and early childhood releases resources that enable us to care for other people and to accept their love in return. These early experiences set us out on the developmental journey that will make us competent lovers.

Attachment theory focuses, then, on the early interaction between parent and child. Behaviors and emotions that are part of the early movements of care-seeking and caregiving are seen as formative. These dynamics set out a framework of how, as adults, we will respond to closeness and separation, to strength and need, to pleasure and injury, to affirmation and antagonism. And these resources will be critical in our efforts to establish and maintain the life-giving commitments of love.

The healthy infant starts out as a good recruiter. Babies have to be successful in drawing the attention of nearby adults and soliciting their effective care. In these early exchanges, children learn that security comes in closeness. When we are close to other people, our needs will be acknowledged and very often met. Even toddlers, who have developed the muscular control needed to stand and walk on their own, still seek safety in a quick return to the caregiver: running back to mother when confronted by a stranger, holding father's hand in a new or dangerous setting.

Care-seeking by the small child evokes responses from attentive adults. Parents and other caregivers try to understand the child's needs and respond in ways that will help. This engaged concern offers protection to the vulnerable child and expands the resourcefulness of the adult caregiver. Other benefits flow as well. In the care of attentive adults, the child learns that exploring inner experience is safe. This empathic interaction helps children develop confidence in the wide range of thoughts and actions that are part of their own awareness, experiences that are mine and me.

As their caregivers call attention to behaviors that are part of the good me and the bad me, children learn that self has many dimensions.

In a nurturing family environment, a child can come to recognize these different qualities without succumbing to denial or shame. Still, many of us as adults face the challenge of accepting those essential dimensions of "who I am" that, in our childhood, were identified as unacceptable or bad. And learning to question those powerful early negative evaluations allows us to welcome more of "who I really am" into our life now.

Successful early attachment brings an additional benefit: the child experiences the world as a welcoming place. Exploring my environment in the presence of loving and protective adults shows me that curiosity is safe. Even when my own resources are limited, even when personal vulnerability leaves me ill-equipped, I do not face the world alone. This confidence expands the range of my life experience. I am more open to novelty and change, free to participate and explore—because there are others I can count on to help cover the risks. These early dynamics of care-seeking and caregiving influence our later openness to close relationships. When we are fortunate, early relationships bring us into adulthood with the resources we need to embrace the adult experiences of love in its many and varied dimensions.

Attachment as an Adult Resource

Adult attachment honors our natural desire for presence and proximity. From earlier experience we've learned that it is good to be close to other people: closeness brings protection, closeness carries delight, closeness strengthens self-esteem. As we mature, we recognize that these gifts of relationships are not always guaranteed. But resources from our early experience allow us to approach new relationships with positive expectations. And what we look for in close relationships is not just protection or help with problem solving. What counts most is the attentive presence of another person. The responses that touch us deeply come not from "just anybody," but from those who are emotionally significant in our lives. We are eager to be connected with people who respond to us—not simply out of pity or a sense of obligation but from the heart.

Adult attachment teaches us that risk and trust are related. In close relationships, vulnerability can be acknowledged and respected. Our weaknesses do not have to remain hidden to protect us from being manipulated or hurt. Here we are free to share more of "who I really am," knowing that our strengths will be welcomed and our limitations will be met with understanding and support. Close adult relationships—both within the family and beyond—bring the gifts of mutuality. Mutuality does not require that we each become the exclusive focus of the other person's concern. But mutuality thrives in our attuned responsiveness to one another. Here we are known "in particular" and loved for who we are. And here the giving and receiving go both ways.

Resources of adult attachment help us be attentive in our relationships—mindful of the movements of our own heart even as we are sensitive to the needs and hopes of those we love. And when our ordinary ways of being together come under stress, when tensions arise that cause us to doubt someone who is close to us, we learn to pay attention to the relationship itself. Acknowledging harm and hurt when these occur, being ready both to seek and to offer forgiveness—these practices strengthen bonds between us that may have been broken. And in mature attachment, it is not just one of us who assumes the tasks of tending to our relationship. This responsibility is shared.

Mature attachment and interdependence are closely related. But the American commitment to *independence* complicates mutuality for many of us. This cultural ideal seems to suggest that interdependence is immature; to depend on someone else is somehow infantilizing for me. This is especially relevant in the experience of American men, but many women are influenced by this cultural prejudice as well. This hesitance surrounding interdependence complicates the development of strong emotional ties, and it works against the development of sustaining relationships.

Mature attachment shows us it is safe to depend on other people. Those closest to me will quickly learn of both my strengths and my limitations. But I am confident they will not take advantage of my vulnerability. Even when those I depend on cannot shield me from pain or distress, I know that their goal is that I may flourish. And I hold them, too, in this privileged embrace of care. Without this shared vulnerability, as Daniel Stern insists, "true intimacy cannot and does not exist."

Appropriate Vulnerability

Close relationships bring us to life; close relationships put us at risk. Most of us want to be open in our relationships—honest, sensitive, available. At the same time we fear being vulnerable. Martha Nussbaum traces links between vulnerability and maturity: "Human beings are deeply troubled about being human—about being highly intelligent and resourceful, on the one hand, but weak and vulnerable, helpless against death, on the other. We are ashamed of this awkward condition and, in manifold ways we try to hide from it." But, Nussbaum insists, these often distressing emotions are "essential and valuable reminders of our common humanity."

Vulnerability threatens when we recognize that we may be hurt. So we try hard to avoid situations where we could be judged inadequate, or where we might be wounded or insulted or abandoned. And experience brings us to an even more sober realization: drawing close to others, it is likely that we will be hurt—we may feel taken for granted, often disappointed, sometimes misunderstood, or, more seriously, perhaps even betrayed.

When sex and sexuality come into play, we are especially vulnerable. In these settings we are exposed—both physically and psychologically. Here we stand revealed in our bodies, our hopes, our desires, our needs. We open ourselves to be strongly affected by someone else and recognize that we may be injured or abandoned. But other settings, too, carry risk. We can be caught in a work situation where our own needs or values are ignored. Or we may become aware of subtle prejudices that are at play in a civic group whose approval is important to us. Or responding to injustice, we may be drawn to take actions that put us at odds with the status quo and place us at risk of public rebuke or social sanctions.

Vulnerability becomes a concern when we sense that sharing our feelings and fears—or our values and convictions—will give other people opportunity to take unfair advantage or to use this information against us. But vulnerability is about more than being hurt; vulnerability is also about being genuinely present. Here vulnerability becomes a resource; we might even speak of vulnerability as a virtue.

As a virtue, vulnerability opens us to life. Wise vulnerability helps us face unresolved feelings, acknowledging the hidden grief that keeps us from moving forward. Befriending vulnerability lets us learn from other people's responses to us rather than simply defend against their candid feedback. Growing comfort with vulnerability supports us in trying out new behavior, taking on new challenges—even when the outcome is unclear.

Personal vulnerability also strengthens close relationships. Coming to accept myself more fully, I am less afraid to share myself with you. This openness allows us to be seen, to be known, to be loved for who we really are. Wise vulnerability allows us to acknowledge our limitations, admit our mistakes, and accept responsibility for hurts we have inflicted on other people—making forgiveness and reconciliation possible.

Vulnerability comes into play in the public arena as well. Paradoxically, accepting our limits often frees us to take action. Being criticized by others becomes less threatening. We don't need guaranteed approval before we take a stand. We are ready to defend views that are out-of-fashion or suggest alternatives that challenge the status quo. We can question majority opinions by asking, "Why?" and "Why not?" These resources support our actions in pursuit of justice, even in the face of opposition.

Psychologist Brene Brown insists that "vulnerability may be at the core of fear and uncertainty, but it is also the birthplace of courage and compassion." Facing my vulnerability takes courage; the world is a dangerous place, and my resources are not always sufficient. Even more, Brown reminds us, it takes courage to be imperfect, to accept myself as I am now. To be sure, "who I am now" is not all that I might be, perhaps not all that I want to be. But befriending my limits strengthens me. Who I am now is enough. And this very acknowledgment leaves me less defensive, less self-protective, more open to change and growth.

Appreciating our own vulnerability also opens us to greater compassion. Empathy expands as we recognize that others are wounded and inconsistent, just as we are. Compassion toward others is rooted in this self-compassion—knowing and accepting myself as limited or flawed, and yet valuable as is, worthy of love and respect. These strengths of compassion lead to greater personal authenticity. We can let go of the often unrealistic imperatives of "who I should be." The struggle to meet false expectations—our own or those of other people—can be set aside. And an enhanced awareness of integrity follows. This openness to be seen for "who I am now" makes mature commitments possible.

Our willingness to be seen is supported by the internal sense that "I am enough." Not perfect, not without flaw, still on the path, open to growth and development, even aware of wounds that continue to need healing. But who I am now is enough for now—to be embraced, affirmed, and loved, even as the journey continues.

Vulnerability, befriended, supports our richer engagement with the world, energizing our investment beyond self-interest and self-protection. And wise vulnerability is the foundation of empathy, opening us to other people's inner lives. We learn what we care about and come to a better sense of how to respond with care.

Befriending our vulnerability gives us more freedom. Hiding personal weaknesses becomes less important. Our goal is not the defended self who will never be hurt, but the resilient self who can live wholeheartedly. In metal, resilience identifies the capacity to return to an original shape after being compressed or bent. Psychological resiliency names our ability to bounce back from the distress and injuries that assault our lives. The resilient self gradually recovers from the hurt, stronger and with more integrity.

Dimensions of Love

Love is both an emotion and an action. These two dimensions are obviously related, but we can distinguish one from the other. In American culture, romantic feelings are at the heart of love. Several strands are woven together in the fabric of contemporary romance. Physical attraction and emotional response are central, often linked with sexual arousal. Romance reinforces our sense of closeness and the desire for even greater union. These experiences assure us that "we fit together well." More than a sexual comment, this conviction acknowledges our heightened awareness of compatibility and congruence. And romance harbors hope: the strong attraction we experience now holds promise for our future together.

Romance often comes as love's ally. But romance does not always keep its promises. Relationships lived out may not live up to our early expectations. This disappointment does not prove that romance is untrustworthy. But we learn that romance is part insight and part illusion.

Images of romance seldom reflect the actual experience of love in long-term relationships. If love is to last, our illusions must be confronted. This demands not the repudiation of romance, but its purification. Through this purification we come to recognize that love embraces more than feelings. As love grows, the well-being of those we love becomes as important to us as our own. We are eager to devote personal resources—time, energy, attention, influence—so that loved ones may flourish. Love matures as our earlier emotional attraction expands to include these cultivated and chosen commitments. In this, our loving reflects the movements of *agape* and *caritas*—the unconditional love that stands at the core of the major religious traditions of the world.

As a character strength, love depends on—and develops—personal resources of intimacy, commitment, fidelity, and devotion. Psychologists see *intimacy* not as a general sense of altruistic goodwill for all humanity, but as the capacity to commit ourselves to *particular* persons, with all the idiosyncrasies and peculiarities involved. This resource helps us respond to the shifting demands in ongoing relationships in ways that do not compromise our sense of personal integrity.

A second psychological resource is *commitment*. Emotions often arouse us to draw near to others, to espouse an important cause, to extend a willing hand. But commitment expands beyond the immediacy of feelings. Commitment claims us for the future, a season that escapes our control. Commitment does not operate like a factory warranty; commitment is less a guarantee than a pledge. In commitment we hold ourselves accountable to do "whatever is necessary" to honor promises made. At first this seems to be a problematic resource. How can I make promises now in the face of all that is unknown—who will I be, who will be with me, what surprises does the future hold? But without this ability to pledge my future based only on what I know now, I will not thrive.

We see the strength of commitment more fully in its absence. A person is attracted to many others. Each is initially alluring, yet soon seems lacking in some way. Here passion leads not to commitment but to disappointment. Finally, the person is left alone.

Commitment matures in the psychological strength of *fidelity*—the ability to sustain these loyalties that have been freely pledged, in the face of inevitable contradictions that arise in any ongoing relationship. Fidelity does not ensure that we will never experience difficulty or conflict in our overlapping lives. Fidelity does not suggest that we will never let one another down. But fidelity makes mature love possible. We learn not only to make promises but to keep them.

This psychological resource stabilizes us so that we can continue to honor our freely pledged loyalty—even acknowledging the complications that are part of our past, the hesitancies that remain active in the present, and the problems that will inevitably confront us in our future together. Here fidelity points to more than sexual exclusivity. In all our significant relationships—marriage, family, friendship, vocational commitments—fidelity plays an important role. With frustrating regularity, we let each other down. But we also learn to begin again, to forgive, and to accept forgiveness. We gradually shed the illusions and expectations that were perhaps previously necessary but now have become burdensome.

The most mature gift of fidelity is its flexibility. We are committed to a person who keeps growing and changing, as do we ourselves. So our fidelity is not just to promises once made but to a shared journey. Along the way we are revealed more deeply to ourselves, even as we continue to learn about our partner. Gradually we recognize that our life's vocation is not a single call but a lifelong conversation with God.

Devotion is the most extravagant blessing born of maturing love. This strength anchors an abiding commitment, rooted in appreciation that someone else's well-being is as important to me as is my own. Here again, we move beyond a general love of humanity. Devotion arises in our relationships with *particular* persons. And devotion expands when the experience is mutual; I, too, am held in this treasured embrace. Even so, the greatest gift of devoted relationships is presence—the promise that we will *be there* for one another, the assurance that we will not be abandoned.

Devotion is love that is *well aged*. In marriage, devotion is the enfleshed affection that survives crisis and change. Accustomed over decades to each other's ways—both the endearing and the maddening—we know each other well. The youthful passion of romance has been transmuted into the tenderness that enjoys growing old together.

Developmental psychology offers a final insight into the significance of love: it is through our relationships that we become fully human. This conviction clarifies an earlier claim, sometimes attributed to Freudian psychology, that reaching full psychological maturity depends on a lifestyle that includes active genital expression. The psychological disciplines today are more circumspect, and more confident, in their claims. Relationships continue to be seen as central in human maturity, and sexual sharing enhances many relationships. But sexual activity itself is not the essential component of human flourishing; what is essential is that we learn to love and be loved.

Additional Resources

In *A Secure Base: Parent-Child Attachment and Healthy Human Development,* John Bowlby offers a comprehensive introduction to attachment theory. For an excellent overview statement, see Daniel Siegel's *The Developing Mind: How Relationships and the Brain Interact to Shape Who We Are.* Robert Karen expands this discussion in *Becoming Attached: First Relationships and How They Shape Our Capacity to Love.*

For discussion of the neurological basis of attachment behavior and its significance in human development and maturing love, see Thomas Lewis, Fari Amini, and Richard Lannon, *Toward a General Theory of Love* and Helen Fisher, *Why We Love: The Nature and Chemistry of Romantic Love.*

In *Daring Greatly: How the Courage to Be Vulnerable Transforms the Way We Live, Love, Parent, and Lead,* Brene Brown discusses research findings and counseling practices that support vulnerability as a resource. Martha Nussbaum examines cultural forces that provoke a sense of vulnerability in *Hiding from Humanity: Disgust, Shame and the Law.*

Daniel Stern's comment on vulnerability appears in his pioneering study of infant development, *The First Relationship: Mother and Child.*

We offer additional biblical and psychological perspectives on the attachment in *Nourishing the Spirit;* see especially chapter 5. For further discussion of the spiritual and psychological dimensions of love, see our *Wisdom of the Body: Making Sense of Our Sexuality.*

Chapter Three

Friendship Comes as a Gift

*I have called you friends because I have made known to
you everything I have heard from my Father.*

—John 15:15

Our everyday lives are filled with acquaintances—the people we meet at work, in the neighborhood, at church. We greet them with civility and even warmth, but we spend little time with them. We know few details of their lives. But sometimes from this crowd of acquaintances something more emerges. By a happy combination of good fortune and personal effort, friends enrich our lives.

Friendship begins in mutual attraction. We enjoy each other's company and like doing things together. As we spend more time together, we dare to break through the surface of our relationship. Venturing beyond the casual companionship—of neighbors, coworkers, pals—we move into the exciting realm of friendship. Close friends know us in ways that go deeper than surface appearances. Friendship depends on this willingness to share aspects of our inner life and self-understanding. Such self-disclosure is the heart of friendship. Our friends touch a part of us that is not generally accessible, often enough not even to ourselves.

Friendship is a rare blessing today. How do we find the time to build the bonds of trust and affection? Where do we gain the confidence to share our heart with another person? How can we escape the deadly patterns that freeze our conversations in superficial repartee? These questions remind us of the difficulty of friendship in American life. Few structures support a continuing relationship between friends. Friendship doesn't have the legal protection—or constraints—of marriage. Most friendships lack the familiar ritual celebrations (shared holidays, birthdays, anniversaries) that reinforce ties within the family. Moreover, we do not even have many shared understandings of what being a "good friend" asks of us.

Friendship depends almost exclusively on the ongoing emotional links between us. This spontaneity is part of friendship's charm. Friends don't have to keep in touch; friends *choose* to spend time together. Our relationship grows and deepens not because it should but because we both genuinely want it to. But this lack of structure can also imperil our relationship. Responsibilities at work or in our marriage and family seem clearer and more compelling than the demands of friendship. The claims of other commitments easily crowd out the time we might spend with friends. Absorbing energy and attention, these concerns leave us drained when we do find time to be together. Friendship then becomes a refreshing diversion from "real life," with no legitimate demands of its own.

Our mobile lives complicate friendship even more. Friendship flourishes when work or living arrangements put us in proximity. But if one of us moves away, the relationship may die. Nothing beyond ourselves exists that we can look to—guidelines, expectations, "rules of the game"— to help us sustain our friendship at a distance.

Yet, in spite of the complications, friendships thrive. Those of us with good friends rejoice in their presence in our lives. Those without friends often sense that something is missing and long to have someone to share life with in this way. Close friendship links us in memory and mutual care. Our close friends open their hearts and their lives to us. And they reveal us to ourselves, showing us more of who we might be and supporting us through seasons of crisis and change.

A relationship with a friend lets us relax our ordinary well-guarded stance. We put aside some of our necessary and even useful defenses. With friends, we don't need always to be strong. And when friends are not frightened by our weaknesses, we learn to be a bit more comfortable with them ourselves. We may even begin to befriend the frailties from which we have, unsuccessfully, tried to hide.

With friends we don't always have to be consistent. This rare freedom lets us explore the contradictions that are part of our inner life. To a friend, we can acknowledge that we are both generous and selfish, sometimes courageous but often enough afraid. The affection of our friends provides a kind of sacred space; here we can explore the parts of life that bewilder us, that challenge us, that seem absurd. Friends help us face the future with less fear.

The Core of Friendship

Friends enrich and expand our lives. But what does friendship do for us? Why is it so special? To answer these questions, psychologists have examined the mutually supportive and intimate relationships that most of us would call close friendships. Close relationships are not all alike. Friendships between women and men, for example, may have different dynamics than those between persons of the same gender. Some friendships are long-standing while others are more short-term. While sexual sharing may be part of a friendship, most often it is not. But more important than these differences among adult friendships is a crucial similarity: as a friendship develops, the partners become *reliable emotional confidants.*

A close friend is, first, a *confidant:* someone with whom we share confidences. We can be open here because we know this person can be counted on, especially in circumstances that involve risk and vulnerability. With a friend, exploring questions that often remained hidden is safe. As a friendship deepens, we let ourselves be influenced—even changed—by someone we love.

Friendship links us as *emotional* confidants. Going beyond the enjoyment of each other's company, we enter into one another's inner life. The bond between us is not based just on common activities or similar tastes; we exchange more than ideas. Friendship includes emotional self-disclosure—direct, immediate conversation about what is going on in our heart and mind. Willingness to talk about thoughts and feelings seems essential to a deepening friendship.

And as friendship grows, we become *reliable* emotional confidants. A history of trust exists between us; we have proved ourselves dependable. This heritage helps us approach one another in confidence: here we will not be mocked; here we will not be judged; here we will not be scorned. Dependability does not mean that we will always agree, nor does it ensure that we will never hurt one another. Sometimes our words and actions cause pain. Dependability doesn't exclude all conflict or confrontation between us: often only a friend is close enough and courageous enough to tell the truth, especially when the truth is hard for us to hear. But in friendship, we come to count on one other to act consistently with openness, understanding, and respect. With a friend, we know that we are *valued* before we are evaluated.

Friendship is so special because these gifts are mutual. The giving and the receiving go both ways. Friendship may be therapeutic, but it is not therapy. In therapy we talk about what is really important to us, but the self-disclosure is necessarily one-sided. The intimate details of the therapist's life are considered out of bounds. This kind of one-way openness would cripple a friendship. Friends *share* their inner worlds— the special successes and confusions that are not easily available to casual acquaintances. This mutuality may be suspended in a time of personal crisis, when all the energy of our friendship is focused on one of us in need. But soon, even in such trying times, we need to reestablish our pattern of mutuality. A friendship that remains one-sided is sure to falter.

The Cost of Friendship

Friendship welcomes us into a world of mutual support and loyalty. Since friends share a sense about what really matters in life, our friends help hold us accountable for living according to what we believe. The presence and support of friends are often critical in times of significant personal change, when our own hopes or goals put us at odds with "the way things are." By their acceptance and affection, our friends help us face the guilt and blame and social pressure that may accompany our efforts to be different.

But friendship can also present obstacles to personal growth. Some friends are supportive only as long as we agree with them. Our pals and buddies love us for who we are, but their affection demands that we stay the same. In their eyes, change threatens our friendship. The support of friends can exert emotional pressure for a conformity that leads to stagnation.

But if our true friends teach us about support, they also instruct us in loyalty. As a friendship deepens, we seek to spend more time with each other. We want to be there when the other person needs us. Loyalty means that we do not abandon our friends in times of stress or distraction.

Promiscuity threatens loyalty—not always at a sexual level. In friendship, promiscuity means succumbing to the temptation to move on when the novelty of a relationship wears off. As the demands of friendship become clearer, loyalty can feel like constraint. New people await us "out there"; new experiences of spontaneity and discovery beckon to us. And these new relationships are free of the messy compromises that come with commitment. Loyalty roots us in a conviction that can outlast these temptations.

Misplaced Loyalty

But even loyalty may be distorted. We have all been in a relationship in which a significant problem appears. Perhaps the other person starts drinking more often and more heavily. We begin to fear for his or her health, as well as the safety of anyone who meets the person on the highway at night! We want to bring up the subject of our friend's drinking, but we're afraid to do so. The threat we feel is twofold. First, our image as a good friend comes under question. *Friends, after all, are supposed to accept one another fully, aren't they? Isn't our love meant to be unconditional? Our friendship shouldn't depend on his acting a certain way, should it? At least not just to please me! Am I just being petty by demanding that he change so that I will feel better?*

A second threat strikes more deeply—the fear of abandonment. *Suppose I bring up the issue of his drinking and my friend responds by turning away from me? I'm not sure I can bear to lose this relationship. I need my friend's attention and affection. I do not want to risk these by challenging his behavior.*

What are we to do? This difficult situation raises disquieting questions: Is there no value for which we will risk a relationship? When does loyalty become something else—an unhealthy collusion or codependent behavior? In some circumstances, loyalty holds a severe challenge: it requires that we confront a friend or lover even at the risk of the relationship. A claim of "being loyal to my values" can, of course, become a ruse that we use to disentangle ourselves from relationships that demand too much of us. But sometimes genuine loyalty compels us to risk the loss of a precious friend.

A second distortion of loyalty can happen in long-lasting relationships. Let us start, though, by recognizing the importance of old friends, those tested companions with whom we have shared decades of life's journey. Friends like this are irreplaceable. We sense this in the special sadness experience at the death of a longtime friend. With this passing we lose part of our own past. However gregarious we remain as we grow older, we cannot make new "old friends." But sometimes old friends can conspire in a kind of perverted loyalty. Gathering to tell old stories and rehearse ancient complaints (about the economy, about the church, about "those others"), we blanket one another in nostalgia; we defend each other against the winds of change. Nostalgia—our delight and absorption in the good old days—is an ordinary and honorable form of grieving. Letting go of old ways of thinking and acting takes time. But eventually we need to let go. When we refuse to change, nostalgia can become chronic. Now a hiding place, our shared past protects us from change and its new demands. Old friends remain good friends when they help us draw strength from the past to face the confusions and possibilities of the future.

Remaking Our Friends

Among the costs of friendship are the surprises and purifications that await us along the way. One of these surprises is our stumbling upon a secret project in some of our friendships: we have been trying to remake the other person, usually in our own image. The early stages of a friendship are often marked by a startling sense of compatibility. Our interests are similar: we like the same music, the same kind of food. Our needs—for privacy, for excitement, for affection—seem to mesh. With delight, we discover that we are not unique or isolated or odd; we find another person *like me* who *likes me*. In a world that showers us with diversity and conflict, this is heady consolation.

Gradually, the two of us come to see that we are not so totally alike. We come slowly upon the foibles and habits that make us different. She is not as punctual as we first thought; he seems more restless than we find comfortable. As our relationship continues, we come upon the maddening habits that stretch our tolerance and remind us of the advantages of solitude.

During this discovery of difference, our secret project is likely to begin. We set out, often unconsciously, to remake the other person. We determine that these minor differences between us can be overcome. With some slight adjustments, we can make our friend "perfect" again! If only we can get him or her to see things our way, we will survive this bumpy period and become lasting friends. We gradually increase the pressure on our friend to change, to be more like us or more like what we need him or her to be.

Then the moment of purification strikes its blow: we come face-to-face with this covert operation. Whether our friend assists us in this discovery or we come upon it on our own, we are shocked. We thought we were above that kind of thing! Now we begin to appreciate the difficulty of a mature friendship. Friendship asks us to let those we love be themselves.

But then the problem deepens: How is this covert remaking different from the proper and necessary ways that friends challenge one another? Are we to become passive and utterly uncritical of each other? Is it that "anything goes"? The answers to these questions will not be found within the privacy of our solitary reflection. Only by bringing the secret project out in the open, by talking about it together, will we find a solution that honors our friendship. We should not feel too ashamed to bring up the topic, since our friend has likely been aware of the project for some time! We need to share our concern with our friend. We need to admit, "I want *this* for you but know I shouldn't force you. What most disturbs you in the agenda of this no-longer-secret project of mine? How can we be more honest with each other?" With effort and candid communication, we can forge the compromises that nurture, rather than destroy, our friendship. We can find more mature ways to be faithful to one another.

Women and Men as Friends

Friendships are a source of solace and challenge for all of us—men and women alike. But recent research has uncovered some intriguing differences in the ways that women and men approach friendship. These are differences in style and in expectation.

The differences in style are more apparent. Men friends *do things together*; women friends *talk things over*. Women value their friendships with other women especially for the understanding and emotional support they receive. Women friends tend to spend time together exploring the inner world of personal experience and meaning. This sharing of thoughts and feelings both expresses and strengthens their emotional bond.

The bond that develops between men friends often has more to do with solidarity than with self-disclosure. Among men, friendship is based more on common experience—at the workplace, in military service, in the neighborhood—than on intimate conversation. As friends, men stand shoulder-to-shoulder more than face-to-face. Confronting a common task, they come in touch with each other. Gradually and indirectly, this association can grow into a deep friendship.

Many men hesitate to discuss their personal life with another man, especially if the conversation might touch on areas of personal weakness or vulnerability. Men often find that expressing strong positive emotions—affection, gratitude, joy—among their men friends is difficult. They rely, instead, on a growing but often unspoken sense of loyalty and camaraderie.

This familiar difference in friendship *style* reflects an underlying difference between women and men in their expectations of friendship. In a close relationship between two men or between two women, the gender difference is not a factor. But as a friendship develops between a woman and a man, this difference in expectations can cause confusion.

Most confusing are expectations about emotional disclosure and sexual attraction. Many women report that a male friend is not as forthcoming as they would like him to be in terms of emotional sharing. Many men indicate that they sometimes feel pressured by a woman friend to reveal more of themselves than is comfortable for them. And men and women agree that, in most cross-gender heterosexual friendships, the issue of sex has to be resolved before the friendship can deepen.

The Erotic Possibilities

Psychologists suggest that these expectations are rooted in our interpretations of the erotic possibilities of friendship. *Eros* includes the full range of attraction and responsiveness that draws people toward one another. This delightful dynamic spans the incredible range of arousals that we experience as embodied persons: the sensual pleasure of a hot bath as well as the emotional companionship of a good friend; the delight of a good meal and the joy of physical lovemaking. But as women and men, we often learn to interpret the erotic possibilities of friendship in quite different ways. In relationships between men and women, these differences come to the fore.

For many men, the erotic possibilities of friendship tend to be understood in explicitly sexual ways. The excitement of a friendship with a woman is closely associated with genital arousal; the "chemistry" that they experience is interpreted as explicitly sexual. Men learn, both from their physiological arousal and from culture, to first ask of this friendship a sexual response. Only as the friendship progresses will they feel safe enough to explore the possibility of emotional intimacy—that deeper sharing of self through significant self-disclosure.

Many women interpret relationships differently. As a friendship begins, most women respond first at the emotional level. They look forward to connecting with this other person in experiences of empathy, care, and companionship. While a woman may be physically attracted to the man who is a potential friend, the emotional attraction she feels toward him is what tells her that friendship is possible here. As the friendship deepens, she may want to include sexual intimacy as part of the relationship. But for most women, emotional closeness comes before and opens the way for genital love. Many men experience these two aspects of *eros* in the reverse order: for them sexual attraction comes before and opens the way to a deeper emotional connection.

This difference in erotic expectations can complicate the efforts of women and men to develop deep friendships with each other. Feeling drawn to a woman, a man may sexualize the relationship in a way that surprises the woman. As she views their relationship, sex is not what brings them together. His obvious sexual interest seems inappropriate and confusing to her. In turn, her disinterest confuses him. He reasons that her reluctance to move the relationship toward genital expression must be because the relationship means less to her than it does to him.

The erotic possibilities of friendship—the opportunities for closeness, affection, mutual support, delight, concern—are vast and complex. As we become more aware of each other's expectations (and our own), we have a better chance of untangling our hopes in friendship. In a particular relationship, we may find the bond of friendship between us expanding to include sex. More often, friendship between women and men thrives in the decision to exclude sexual sharing.

American culture further complicates friendships between women and men. Its bias, evident in the media and other forms of popular culture, suggests that affection between a man and a woman always and inevitably leads to genital expression. Because of this bias, we suspect our own friendships. We begin to second-guess ourselves: *If we really like each other, we ought to be sleeping together, or at least struggling with the question. Maybe we are not being honest with one another.* Both history and personal experience testify to the reality of significant emotional relationships in which genital sexuality has no part. Attraction and affection are strong, as are mutual concern and care. But the communion of these friendships does not include sexual sharing. Another sign of our culture's preoccupation with sex is that we must reassure one another that such a friendship is possible.

Additional Resources

In *Friendships Don't Just Happen*, Shasta Nelson stresses the importance of close relationships in the lives of adults today. Roger Horchow and Sally Horchow offer practical suggestions for developing supportive connections in adult life; see *The Art of Friendship*. Marla Paul addresses factors that complicate friendship in *The Friendship Crisis: Finding, Making, and Keeping Friends*.

Nicole Way examines *Boys' Friendships and the Crisis of Connection*; Sandy Sheehy explores women's experience in *Connecting: The Enduring Power of Female Friendship*.

Pastor Alan Loy McGinnis provides inspiring encouragement and practical advice in *The Friendship Factor*. In *Friendship: A Way of Interpreting Christian Love*, Liz Carmichael examines friendship as a central model of love in Christian tradition.

Chapter Four

The Meanings of Marriage: Promises to Keep

On that day, says the LORD, you will call me, "my husband" ... And I will take you for my wife forever; I will take you for my wife in righteousness and in justice, in steadfast love and in mercy.

—Hosea 2:16, 19

The word *marriage* refers to many things. We can use the word to name our own experience of the day-to-day relationship we share. The word can also designate the social institution of matrimony, which has a legal definition and rights and duties that are regulated by the state and sanctioned by many religious traditions through special rites and ceremonies. Between these two senses of the word—marriage in my experience and marriage as a social institution—there are other meanings as well. Marriage is a relationship, marriage is a commitment, marriage is a lifestyle.

When we speak of marriage as a *relationship*, we focus on the quality of the bond that exists between us, our mutual love. This *commitment* of marriage refers to the promises we make to do "whatever is necessary" to deepen and develop this love and, through this love, to move beyond ourselves in creativity and care. The *lifestyle* of marriage describes the patterns that we develop as we attempt to live out these promises—our choices among values and activities, our patterns in the use of time and money and the other resources we have. These three facets of marriage are overlapping and interrelated. Each contributes richly to the complexity of our life together and to the satisfaction we experience in marriage. And as we are becoming more aware, none of the aspects of our marriage is ever finished or static. Each is in movement, in an ongoing process of realization and development—or decline.

The Relationship of Marriage: Mutual Love

The expectations of love in marriage today are high. The *ideal* of married love for most people includes romance, sex, friendship, and devotion. Romance: we want the emotion and physical attraction that we experience early in our relationship to continue through our married years. Sex: we want our lovemaking to be lively and mutually satisfying, enhanced by deepening responsiveness to each other's preferences and needs. Friendship: we want to continue to like each other, to enjoy each other's company, to find in each other the sources of comfort and challenge, of solace and stimulation that we need for continuing growth. Devotion: we want to be able to *count on* one another, to give our trust in the deep conviction that it will not be betrayed, to experience the awesome responsibility and transforming power of holding someone else's well-being as important to us as our own and to know that we, too, are held in such care.

These are not easy accomplishments. With these high expectations come equally high demands. In a relationship that is mutual, we must be ready to give these benefits as well as to receive them. And for many of us, these emotional benefits are sought and expected only in marriage. We have no other so serious and so sustained an adult relationship.

Marriage did not always carry such high emotional demands. In earlier generations, wives and husbands did not usually become one another's chief companion or best friend. Each could be expected to develop a range of social relationships—in the extended family, in the neighborhood, in the workplace, in clubs and churches and associations—that provided support and a sense of belonging to complement the marriage relationship. Today our involvement in these wider circles seems to have slipped. Economic and geographic mobility can cut into, even cut off, ties with family and neighborhood. The workplace is increasingly competitive; our relationships there seem of necessity to remain superficial. No one wants to take the risk of deeper friendship with a potential rival. And here, too, mobility plays a part in keeping those relationships light. We know it is likely that one or both of us may move to another job. Many associations—political parties, civic groups, churches—seem to have lost the consensus they formerly enjoyed. In these groups today, we are likely to experience polarization rather than a sense of belonging.

Now it is often only from our spouse and, perhaps, our children that we expect any deep or continuing emotional response. This expectation has enriched the experience of mutuality in marriage, but it has also added to its strain. There are few of us today who would choose a style of marriage that did not include friendship and mutuality among its chief goals. But we do not often give much attention to the pressures that are inevitable in the companionate marriage or to the resources that may be required for us to live well in this style of mutual love.

Marriage brings us in touch with our incompatible hopes for human life. It is useful to look at some of these tensions and ambiguities that are inevitable as we attempt to live as complex a relationship as marriage. These tensions exist not simply because I am "selfish" or my spouse is "unreasonable" or "immature." These tensions are built into the experience of relationship—most relationships, but especially relationships as multifaceted as marriage.

Security and adventure are both significant goals in adult life. We seek the stability of established patterns, yet we are attracted by the new and the unknown. Often we sense these goals in opposition; life seems to force our choice of one over the other. To seek adventure means to risk some of the security we have known; to be secure means to turn away from some of life's invitations to novelty and change. Most of us learn to make these choices, but our ambivalence remains. At times when the pull of security is strong, change may be uninviting or even dangerous. A preference for stability will seem easy to sustain. But at other times the appeal of change will be compelling and stability will seem like a synonym for boredom and stagnation.

One of the ongoing tensions of marriage concerns this conflict between freedom and security, adventure and stability. I want to deepen the love and life we share, and I want to be able to pursue other possibilities that are open to me, unencumbered by the limits that come with my commitment to you. I need change and novelty and challenge; I also yearn for what is predictable and familiar and sure. I want to be close to you in a way that lets me share my weaknesses as well as my strengths, and I want to be strong enough to stand apart from you and from the relationship we share. Again, the presence of these incompatibles is not, of itself, cause for concern. These are normal, expectable, inevitable. But, then, neither is it surprising that the process of mediating among these needs generates considerable stress.

The commitment of marriage takes us to the heart of this ambivalence between stability and change. In marriage we say both yes and no to the possibilities that our life together will include. Marriage for a lifetime demands both stability (that we hold ourselves faithful to promises we have made) and change (that we recognize the shifting context in which our promises remain alive). We can anticipate that at different points in our marriage we will experience ambivalence—sometimes celebrating the new developments in our life together, sometimes resisting these changes; sometimes grateful for the stability of our love, sometimes resenting its predictability.

Marriage invites me to recognize these ambiguities of my heart as I attempt a style of life and love in which I can both express myself and hold myself accountable. Without commitment and choices, I know I remain a child, but that realization seldom makes choosing any easier.

The Commitments of Marriage: Priority and Permanence

The commitments of marriage are the promises we make. In many ways it is these promises that transform our early attraction into marriage—an enduring relationship of mutual love and shared life-giving. Both by our choice and by the momentum of its own dynamics, marriage projects us beyond the present. Through the hopes we hold for our life together, we condition the future—we begin to mold and shape it. We open ourselves to possibilities, we make demands, we place limits, we hold one another in trust.

Our commitments, of course, do not control the future. We learn this mighty lesson as we move through adult life, invited by the events of our days to give up, one by one, our adolescent images of omnipotence. An illusory sense of the degree to which we can control our own destinies may have once served us well, energizing us to move beyond indecision and enter the complex world of adult responsibility. But we know now that we are both stronger and weaker than we had earlier anticipated. Our promises are fragile, but they still have force. It is on the vulnerable strength of human commitment that we base our hope. And it is through our commitments that we engage the future.

The commitments of marriage are the promises we make—to ourselves, to one another, to the world beyond—to do "whatever is necessary" so that the love we experience may endure, even more that it may flourish. Our own relationship of love is, we know, similar to that which other couples share. But it is in many ways special, unique to who we are, peculiar to the strengths and needs and history we have. Our commitment, then, will reflect features in common with most marriages as well as the demands and possibilities that are particularly our own.

Two of the commitments that have been seen to be at the core of marriage are sexual exclusivity and permanence. The social meaning of these commitments has fluctuated across time. Stress on the importance of the woman's virginity at marriage and her sexual availability only to her husband after marriage is particularly strong in cultures where property and social status are transferred according to the male line of descent. It is important here that there be no confusion about paternity. And strict regulation of the woman's sexual experience is one way to keep the facts of paternity clear.

In many marriages today, couples experience their sexual exclusivity as an expression of more encompassing bonds of mutual commitment. Spouses hold priority in each other's lives, influencing each other's decisions and actions. Every marriage must come to terms with these two dimensions of commitment: our expectations of exclusivity (What is the meaning of the priority in which we hold each other in love? How is this priority expressed?) and our expectations of permanence (What is the significance of our hope that our love shall flourish for our lifetime? How does this hope influence our lives now?).

The Lifestyle of Marriage

Marriage celebrates love, and marriage includes commitment; marriage also creates a lifestyle—not a single lifestyle experienced universally but many particular lifestyles through which married couples express their love and live out the promises that hold them in mutual care.

The lifestyle of marriage is the design or pattern of our life together, emerging in the choices we make. Many people do not experience the patterns of their daily life as open to personal choice. By the time of marriage, and long before, factors of poverty or class or personality have narrowed the range of those parts of life over which they have much say. But most Americans today experience a heightened consciousness of choice. We are aware that there are different ways in which the possibilities of marriage may be lived out. And while our choices are always limited, we are aware that we not only can but must choose among these options. The lifestyle of our marriage thus results from both our choices and our circumstances.

The choices that construct the lifestyle of our marriage include decisions we make about the practical details of living—the routine of our daily activities, how we allocate the current tasks of family and household care. But more basic decisions are involved—the values we hold important, the goals we have for our life together, the ways we choose to invest ourselves in the world.

At the heart of our decisions about lifestyle are certain questions: What is our marriage for? Are we married only for ourselves? Does our life together exist chiefly as a place of personal security and a source of mutual satisfaction? Or is our marriage also about more than just the two of us? Is it a way for us to engage ourselves—together—in a world that is larger than ourselves?

In previous decades, the expected presence of children in marriage answered this question in part. One of the things our marriage is for is our children. A child is so concrete an expression of the love that exists between us and so insistent an invitation that this love extend beyond "just us" in care. In parenting we experience the scope of our love expanding to include our children. Often this broadening of concern continues, to include more of the world and even the future, in which "our children's children" shall have to find their own way. Married people have always been generously engaged in the world in ways other than as parents. But the central connection between being married and having children has been so clear and so prevalent for centuries that it has been a defining characteristic of the lifestyle of marriage.

Today more choice is involved in the link between marriage and parenthood. Couples come to the decision to have a child with more consideration given to how many children shall be in the family, how the birth of these children shall be spaced, when in marriage the commitments of family life shall begin. Some couples who have been unable to give birth to children seek other ways to expand their life together as a family—through adoption or foster care or through the assistance of developments in the fertility sciences and medical practice. Other couples decide not to have a family and instead to express their love beyond themselves in other forms of creativity and care.

A comparable challenge accompanies each of these options—to develop a way of being together in marriage that takes seriously the demands of mutuality in our own relationship as it takes seriously the challenge that we look beyond ourselves in genuine contribution and care. Thus a central choice in marriage concerns our progeny. How shall we give and nurture life: In our own children? In friendship and other close relationships? In our creative work? In our generous concern for the world? And the decisions that we come to here do much to determine the design of our daily life together.

Beyond this central choice concerning the focus of our creative love, there are other decisions about lifestyle. How shall we use the resources we possess? How, especially, do we allocate our money and our time? Here again the questions can be stated simply: What is our money for? What has priority in our time? We can respond to these questions at the practical level, offering the balance sheet of the family budget and our calendar of weekly events. But as an issue in lifestyle the question goes more to the core: How are our own deepest values expressed or obscured in the lifestyle we embrace?

Most American families today experience both money and time as scarce. There is not enough of either to go around. We have little discretionary income and even less "free" time. There always seem to be more possibilities, more demands than we feel we can meet. But among the demands that seem both genuine and inevitable, there are others that seem to squander us uselessly, leaving us no time to be together or to be at peace and leaving us few resources to use for any purpose beyond ourselves. This sense of overextension characterizes the lifestyle of many marriages. Its prevalence invites us to reflect on our own patterns of allocating money and time—not looking to praise or blame but trying to come to a better sense of the motives and pressures that move us and, in that way, define our lives.

How much does our use of money and time revolve around "just us" as a couple or a family as opposed to "those others"? What are the ways in which our decisions about time and money are more reflective of what our society expects than of the values and activities and possessions that make sense to us? Couples and families will differ in their responses to these questions, as they will differ on other issues of values and lifestyle. But this reflection can lead to a greater congruence between the goals we have for our marriage and the ways that our life is lived on a day-to-day basis.

Establishing our lifestyle in marriage is not done once and for all; this is itself an ongoing process. The lifestyle of our marriage must respond to the movements of development and change in each of us, in our relationship, and in our responsibilities. Marriage for a lifetime, then, develops through the interactions of our relationship, our commitments, and our lifestyle. Our mutual love is at the core of marriage. But in marriage we experience our relationship as more than just our mutual love here and now.

Loving for a Lifetime

While the commitment of marriage matures into a love that is larger than romance, it remains a love in which sexuality and affection are central. We approach sexual maturity in our marriage as we develop our capacity for sharing sexual affection and genital pleasure. This sexual maturity too is more a process than a state. We learn to be good lovers, and for most of us this takes time.

To give ourselves to the process of sexual maturing, we must each be able to move beyond the experience of love play and intercourse as chiefly competitive—an experience of proving myself as a *real* woman or man, or "winning out" over my partner. These interpretations of sex keep the focus on me, making mutuality difficult. And without mutuality, sex is more often a barrier to—rather than a part of—the larger psychological experience of intimacy.

In contrast with many marriages of earlier generations, couples today generally approach marriage with greater awareness of their own bodies and with more information about genital sex. This sophistication is a boon to marriage, but more as a starting point in a satisfying sexual life together than its guarantee. Married sex is a process through which we both learn to contribute to what is, for us, mutually satisfying shared sexual experience. We learn the physical and emotional nuances that make lovemaking special for us. We discover the ways in which passion and affection, humor and intensity, are part of our own love life.

The exhilaration of sexual discovery is usually strong early in marriage. Loving me in my body, you invite me beyond shame and guilt I may still carry. With you I am free to explore my passion and to expose my vulnerability and self-doubt. Having risked the self-revelation of sex—and survived—we can approach with greater confidence the other, even more threatening, process of self-disclosure upon which the quality of our life together will depend.

After an initial period of exploration, our sexual life may begin to level off. We have found a pattern that works for us, and especially in the press of our other responsibilities, this pattern can become routine. It may be only gradually that we realize that though our love is strong, our lovemaking somehow falls short. Our early sexual sharing was surrounded with an aura of romance. Frequently this romantic aura made our experiences of sex more satisfying than our lovemaking skills would otherwise justify! Now sex seems to have lost its savor. We know that the substance of our love is more significant than our sexual style. But paying attention to the ways we hold one another—physically as well as emotionally and spiritually—strengthens the lifelong bonds of love.

Moving from "We Are" to "We Care"

Marriage involves balancing the tensions between our intimacy as a couple and the larger responsibilities of our lives. The challenge is to expand the scope of our effective concern. The birth of our first child can be an early challenge. Here we may experience some strain as we learn to expand beyond ourselves as a couple, in ways that that do not erode the commitments of mutuality between us. Job responsibilities and career choices also raise a challenge. Does marriage mean that only one of us may pursue a career? How do I, how do we, manage the multiple demands of being responsible citizen, financial provider, parent, and spouse? The question can surface as an issue of social concern. How do we balance our commitments to each other and to our children alongside our responsibility to the needs of the world?

Love is creative beyond itself, and it must be so if it is to endure. A love that does not open us to wider concerns risks becoming a caricature of intimacy. It is true that there is often a stage of mutual absorption in love, especially in the early experience of romance. The lovers are enthralled with each other. Everything about the other person is engrossing, and there is little beyond this relationship itself that seems worthy of attention. Job responsibilities, school activities, other friends, and family all pale to insignificance. In this timeless present of romance, *you and I* are all there is.

The world tends to be tolerant of this attitude in lovers, at least for a while. Recalling our own experience with romance, we overlook much of the bizarre behavior of other people in love, and we excuse the rest. We know this shared obsession is but a phase of romance; soon it passes. The romance may mature into a deeper love, or it may die from lack of any further substance. But in either case, the charmed circle of exclusive fascination will be broken. Soon the lovers will rejoin us—better, we trust, for the experience.

This early exclusive focus in love is normal, an important dynamic of the process of exploration and self-disclosure that contributes to the possibility of commitment. But maturing love moderates this exclusivity. Being *for* one another does not require that we have no concern for anyone else. Indeed, the enrichment we experience in being for one another leads us to be for more than *just us*. Our love gives us more of what is best in each of us. We feel the impetus to move beyond ourselves, to share this wealth, to bring others into the power of what our love has given us. This movement of expansion is an expectable dynamic of love as it matures.

Psychologists are aware of the importance to our love of this impulse beyond ourselves. They warn that the absence of any movement beyond "just us" imperils a love relationship. A "pseudo-intimacy" can result, turning the partners in upon themselves in ways that gradually impoverish the relationship. What results from this failure to expand our concern is not an intimacy more protected and complete, but stagnation. This truth about love does not come as news to our religious tradition. Love that does not give life beyond itself will die; Christian wisdom has long proclaimed this sometimes fleeting insight from our own experience. There is an essential connection between loving and giving life. It is this abiding truth that the church tries to share in its celebration of the fruitfulness of marriage.

But in our history there has been a tendency to understand this connection in an almost exclusively biological sense—that every act of genital love must be open to the creation of a child, that bearing children is the most important goal of marriage and married love. Many Catholics today, especially married people, find these statements of the connection between marriage and generative love to be at odds with their own experience. But the larger truth, that a maturing love in marriage both wants to and needs to go beyond itself, is reinforced by experience and by religious heritage.

Additional Resources

Julie Rubio explores the theology and spirituality of marriage and family life in *A Christian Theology of Marriage and Family* and in *Family Ethics: Practices for Christians*. Richard Gaillardetz contributes to these themes in *A Daring Promise: A Spiritualty of Christian Marriage*.

Todd Salzman, Thomas Kelly, and John O'Keefe present a significant group of essays in *Marriage in the Catholic Tradition: Scripture, Tradition, and Experience*. Michael Lawler continues the discussion in *Marriage in the Catholic Church: Disputed Questions;* see also his article "Becoming Married in the Catholic Church: A Traditional Post-Modern Proposal," *Intams Journal*.

For further consideration, see David Thomas's *Christian Marriage: The New Challenge* and *Perspectives on Marriage,* edited by Kieran Scott and Michael Warren. In *Let's Make Love,* Jack Dominian offers a sensitive exploration of married love, with a theological reflection on sexual intercourse. Adrian Thatcher's *Celebrating Christian Marriage* explores themes of Christian marriage in cross-cultural perspective.

Chapter Five
Christian Practices: Self-Care and Mindfulness

*You shall love the Lord your God with all your heart, and
with all your soul, and with all your mind, and with all
your strength ... You shall love your neighbor as yourself.*
—Mark 12:30, 31

Christians have traditionally understood virtues as mental attitudes or spiritual states. Many persons today are envisioning virtues as practices—as "what we do." Practices are chosen ways of behaving, regularly repeated actions that form our moral character and shape our identity. Practices locate virtue in everyday life, expressing our "habits of the heart."

Practices are deliberate behaviors. For example, the athlete's commitment to soccer practice or an individual's practice of yoga—these are not random events or mindless habits but chosen activities. For many, weekly attendance at an AA or Al-Anon meeting serves as an essential spiritual practice. Practices, then, are purposeful actions. Part of their purpose is to establish links with important value systems. So we speak of a physician's medical practice or the attorney's practice of law. These professional activities connect the *practitioner* with something larger than just him- or herself—for the physician, a tradition of healing; for the attorney, a heritage of justice.

Similarly, spiritual practices put us in touch with religious traditions, tested legacies that connect us with the wisdom of communities of faith that have preceded our own. Practices shape us through chosen behaviors that guide us toward valued goals. These personal activities form and transform the self. Spiritual practices, as Aaron Stalnaker notes, "aim at a complete transformation of vision, a metamorphosis of the whole personality."

Self-Love: An Essential Practice

The insight guiding our reclamation of the virtue of self-love is rooted in the Gospel's great commandment. Here we are summoned to three loves: we are to love God above all and to love our neighbor *as ourselves* (Mark 12:30). Moral theologian James Keenan is among the first to endorse the practice of self-love—which he identifies as self-care—as an essential virtue for Christians. In his reframing of the cardinal virtues of prudence, justice, fortitude, and temperance, Keenan argues for a threefold regard for others and ourselves. Justice governs our dealing with all others; it is impartial and universal. The virtue of fidelity guides our more immediate relationships with those to whom we have pledged enduring commitments; its focus is more limited and particular. The virtue of self-care supports the respect and trust of ourselves that underpins all our efforts of love and work, of fidelity and justice.

Keenan identifies self-care as an essential virtue in our sexual lives and beyond. The virtue of self-care "brings with it an ability to not let oneself be taken advantage in any relationships, sexual or otherwise." Self-care reminds us that we are responsible for ourselves in our sexual relationships as well as elsewhere in our lives. And this virtue invites us to be as patient with our own confusion and missteps as we are with those of others.

Keenan recognizes that "a self-care informed by mercy prompts us to attend to our own personal histories where areas of need or particular vulnerability need to be recognized rather than repressed." The virtue of self-care strengthens our appreciation of sexuality as part of our graced identity.

Theologians Michael Lawler and Todd Salzman also explore the importance of self-love. They focus on "a self-love that empowers me to understand myself and my right place in those real relationships, and inserts me justly and lovingly into those relationships, is as virtuous as any love of neighbor and is, indeed, a necessary precondition for genuine neighbor-love." And they conclude, "[I]f persons do not fully accept themselves, in both their wholeness and brokenness, neither can they give themselves fully to another person or fully accept that other person."

Ethicist Julie Hanlon Rubio considers self-love as essential in sustaining the commitments of marital love. She honors the traditional understanding that love often demands self-sacrifice, but she also insists that healthy self-regard and self-care are even more essential to marriage and family life. In discussing the practices of lovemaking in marriage, Rubio argues that "when rightly understood as intimately related to the traditional good of union, self-love can be recognized as an essential dimension of good sexual practice." Rubio concludes that "sex that is not grounded in self-love is not likely to be fully giving or fully unifying, while sex that begins in self-love is likely to be better on both counts." In Rubio's analysis, self-care and concern for another come together: "Good sexual practice must include both seeking pleasure and receiving it, along with attending to one's partner's needs to do the same."

Practicing the Love of Oneself

Psychologists, too, have explored the significance of self-love, focusing on two dimensions: self-regard and self-care. *Self-regard* is a positive appreciation of oneself that supports a sense of self-worth. *Self-care* points to the practical ways in which we act to protect and respect ourselves.

A sense of self-worth is rooted in an inner dialogue, one that often functions outside conscious awareness. We become more aware of the inner dialogue by paying attention to our *self-talk*. Self-talk names the internal messages, not explicitly conscious, that we give ourselves throughout the day. Self-talk supplies a background chatter of self-evaluation, often echoing the voices of others—parents and other family members, important teachers and mentors, even the bullies and bosses from our past. This echo chamber is not always accurate, but it is always significant. Self-talk reflects our beliefs, reinforces our feelings, and shapes our behavior.

Cultivating self-regard demands an effort to become aware of the characteristic ways in which we evaluate ourselves. For many of us, negative messages prevail: "There I go again; clumsy me," or "I always make a fool of myself when I try something new," or "It's just selfish of me, or impractical, or dangerous to ask for what I need here." Looking at our response to compliments can be helpful, too. Do we allow time to savor these confirming remarks, by dwelling in the positive feelings they evoke? Or are we more likely to deny this affirmation, canceling any good feelings that might arise, with the result that the lingering judgment that "I'm not good enough" goes unchallenged.

Forming and following personal conscience also reinforces positive self-regard. We respect and feel good about ourselves when our behavior matches our professed values. Even when "doing the right thing" is difficult, conscientious behavior enhances a positive sense of self.

Self-regard supports an inner dialogue that reinforces a sense of self-worth. For Christians, self-regard is grounded in gratitude, our response to the original blessing of being loved by God for who we are. And this positive self-regard supports our commitments to self-care.

Self-Care as Practice and Virtue

Self-care includes in its scope the well-being of the whole person—body, mind, and spirit. Many of us see our bodies as deficient, failing to meet the criteria of beauty or performance that our culture celebrates. We castigate ourselves as too heavy, too frail, too awkward. An essential movement of self-care is self-acceptance—welcoming my body as mine, as me. My body then becomes an honored conversation partner in the decisions I make about diet, rest, work, recreation. We pay more attention to our physical well-being. Conscious of what good health demands, we include physical exercise in our weekly schedule, or we begin the regular practice of yoga or tai chi. Or we adopt the practical discipline of monitoring the amount of caffeine and alcohol and sugar we consume.

Becoming more intentional about food may also lead to our adopting a practice of periodic fasting—not to punish the body or deprive the soul but to help us become more aware of the role of food in our life, more appreciative of those who provide and prepare nourishment. Periodic fasting may also help us become mindful of those throughout the world who regularly lack access to sufficient food for themselves and their families.

Giving thought to what our body requires and developing a lifestyle that honors these needs, we lay a foundation for self-care. As we become more intentional about our physical well-being, these thoughtful practices become part of our spiritual mindfulness as well as central in our commitment to good health. Bringing the body more explicitly into prayer deepens the reverence of self-care. Graceful movement, music and song, colorful banners and incense, icons and other works of art: these sensual expressions can deepen, rather than distract from, an awareness of God's presence and purpose in our life.

Self-care also supports a greater appreciation of our interior life, the spacious inner world of ideas, hopes, longings, values. Through formal study or informal reading, through clarifying our value commitments or devoting time to savoring the arts, we learn to take our inner life seriously. We open ourselves to the experiences of beauty and joy that come as unexpected gifts. We learn to savor pleasure and delight.

This spiritual practice often requires the asceticism of saying no. Our own needs have a valid claim on our time, on our resourcefulness. So sometimes we must put limits on our availability to other people, even those we love. And experience shows that our no is often enough a gift to these others, inviting them to greater personal responsibility, leaving space for them to take action on their own.

Self-care encourages us to recognize our abilities. Our talents—however modest these sometimes seem!—are gifts from God. In humility, we acknowledge that the Spirit sometimes works through our weaknesses. But genuine humility also calls us to delight in our particular gifts and to use them well. Our talents and creativity are the foundation of our vocation. With them we make our contribution to the common good; through them we find ways to serve God's reign of justice and peace. Self-care, then, includes our commitment to develop our personal resources, the skills and strengths through which we express our personal power and contribute to the well-being of the world.

Self-care makes room for friendship and love. Our close friends appreciate aspects of *who we are* not easily accessible to other people, sometimes not even to ourselves. As love deepens, we come to count on one another for affection, understanding, and respect. These life-sustaining relationships come as gifts, but they are not "free." Loving well makes demands. Friendships take time: time to develop, time to maintain, time to reestablish after hurt or harm. Spending time with our loved ones, making time for our friends—these are essential disciplines of self-care. Learning to take care of our close relationships enriches us.

Self-care encourages us to embrace passion and desire. Spiritual writers and psychologists alike locate passion at the root of our vitality, supporting both creativity and commitment. Philip Sheldrake insists that desire invigorates the spiritual journey. Robert Bly urges us to "nurture our tiny desires" as reliable signposts guiding us toward personal integrity. Keenan reinforces this conviction: "I consider the most important task of self-care to be the formation of one's own conscience, for in that we respond to the God who calls us."

This practice sometimes demands our overcoming the effects of earlier socialization that have wounded our self-confidence and left us distrustful of desire. We may have learned that our instincts are unreliable, that passion is likely to lead to actions that threaten moral integrity or distract from the life of the spirit. As we recognize these attitudes as malpractice, self-care may lead us to seek out a setting of healing—a pastoral counselor, a twelve-step support group, a psychological therapist—in which these ingrained patterns of self-defeating behavior can be confronted. Here we may learn again (or for the first time) that our passion can be trusted. Then our emotions themselves become resources in our ongoing discernment of the spiritual path ahead.

Honoring these commitments to self-care will make demands on our time and energy. Many people today find that the middle years hold opportunity for a midcourse realignment. Challenged by failure or frustration or even by previous success, adults at this point in life often face the daunting question of is this all there is? The mood here does not necessarily involve disappointment or discrediting the past. But for some there is an invigorating sense of future possibilities, a new openness to risk taking. Self-care in this setting demands time spent in revisiting earlier life dreams, in realistic assessments of current strengths and limits, in recommitment to the future that still holds promise.

The Practice of Mindfulness

For some Christians, mindfulness suggests a New Age strategy that has little to do with the life of faith. In fact, the practice of mindfulness has deep roots in the Christian heritage. At its heart, mindfulness is an effort to live less distracted—to hold ourselves more thoroughly open to the presence of God. Mindfulness is "the awareness that arises when paying attention on purpose, in the present moment, non-judgmentally, to things as they are … Being mindful means intentionally turning off the autopilot mode in which we operate so much of the time" (*The Mindful Way through Depression*).

This practice is especially suited for the *interval* times in our lives— time spent waiting at the doctor's office, on public transportation, or sitting on the airport runway before takeoff. During these "down" times, our mind tends to wander; we page through the month-old magazines in the waiting room; we observe other passengers on the bus or train. Fears, worries, regrets tumble through our mind in great disarray as we wait for our life to continue. But there is another way to navigate these intervals. In an effort to be more present to our lives, we can simply close our eyes and begin slow and conscious breathing, perhaps adding a brief calming phrase or prayer. Instead of trying to distract ourselves, we choose to be present—in our body, at this moment, in this place.

Mindfulness is a cultivated ability to observe ourselves calmly, to become aware of the feelings coursing through our mind and the tensions present in our bodies. Mindfulness includes attunement to the signals and alerts arising within our physical frame and nervous system—what we might call the wisdom of the body. A practiced attention to our bodily self—performed with compassion and without criticism or judgment— frees us to live with greater focus and joy.

The practice of mindfulness alerts us not only to our own experience but to the moods and needs of those around us. This attentive effort supports the healing attitude of compassion. Hanh and Cheung emphasize this compassionate side of mindfulness. "When we are mindful, touching deeply the present moment, in the here and now, we gain more understanding, more acceptance, more forgiveness and love of self and others; our aspiration to relieve suffering grows; and we have more chance to touch joy and peace."

The Ignatian Examination of Consciousness

The practice of spiritual exercises has a long pedigree in Western culture. In the ancient world, philosophy was understood as a disciplined approach to "the art of living." The goal of its systematic pursuit was practical wisdom more than theoretical certainty. Influential Stoic thinkers Seneca and Marcus Aurelius, for example, developed a range of practices intended to control and shape the emotions. Their intent was, Pierre Hadot argues, "a therapeutic of the passions," which were seen as "unregulated desires and exaggerated fears."

Spiritual exercises today alert us to the movements of grace that energize the spiritual journey and strengthen us to confront obstacles along the way. Many of us are familiar with *The Spiritual Exercises,* a series of meditations and reflections developed by Ignatius Loyola in the sixteenth century. In this retreat format, Ignatius recruited imagination and emotion to focus the heart on living a grateful and generous Christian life. At the core of the *Spiritual Exercises* is the daily practice of an *examen*—an examination of conscience or, better, an examination of our consciousness. Often practiced in both morning and evening, this exercise of mindfulness helps a person reflect prayerfully on the events of the day—as it begins and as it comes to a close. The intent is neither self-accusation nor self-absorption, but greater presence to our lives. Whether we respond with thanksgiving or with regret, the goal of this effort is personal integration.

In *The Ignatian Workout: Daily Spiritual Exercises for a Healthy Faith,* Timothy Muldoon sets out a contemporary model of this schema, outlining the movements that shape this spiritual practice. Before the day begins in earnest, a person takes some moments to become more aware of God's immediacy and presence. As Muldoon suggests, "pray that God might help you understand how God is working with you in your everyday life." Next comes some attention to the events that will fill out the day ahead. "Begin in thankfulness for the basic blessings—being alive, the people you love, your family, your work. And ask for God's help with any difficulties confronting you these days."

In the next moment of this practice, focus shifts to any strong feelings that now arise—whether emotions of anticipation or anxiety or regret. The goal is not to censure but to acknowledge and simply be present. From this array of emotions, the person might choose one for further reflection. This might take the shape of simply giving thanks for the feeling or asking God's help in overcoming this feeling, or expressing willingness to be open to God's presence in this emotion. The morning exercise concludes with a prayer of gratitude.

Similarly, in a moment of quiet at the end of the day (many practice this reflection before dinner), a person becomes attentive to the day's many events. A prayer of thanks for the delights and graces of the day follows. Then, again, the focus may turn to a strong emotion of the day—anger or impatience or compassion. The goal here is not to render judgment but simply to be present to the events that stirred the emotion. Muldoon suggests a gentle questioning: "How was this experience troublesome— disturbing or challenging? How was this feeling confirming for you— consoling or comforting? How did this experience of passion come to you as grace?" The goal is not to "solve" the day's problems or "resolve" some complex emotion. The intent is simply to be more aware of the day's movement and more conscious of the emotional forces that arise on a daily basis. The practice concludes with a prayer of thanks.

The Buddhist Exercise of Bare Attention

The Buddhist practice of bare attention is a meditative means of holding a powerful emotion—anger or loneliness or shame—in attention, without being overwhelmed or distracted by the many fearful associations that we attach to these feelings. Mark Epstein, an American psychiatrist and practitioner of Buddhist meditation, offers background information on this practice: "According to Buddhism, it is our fear at experiencing ourselves directly that creates suffering." It is not our painful emotions themselves that terrify us, but the negative judgments and frightful associations that surround these feelings.

We all recall the "frightful associations" that sometimes accompany ordinary feelings like fatigue or hunger. As we begin to feel tired, assessments of our weakness and inadequacy begin to multiply in our mind. *Why am I so tired? I should be stronger. Other people don't feel tired like this.* This self-criticism—of which we are seldom fully conscious—adds to our fatigue, producing a truly negative emotion. Or we experience the first pangs of hunger and feel a slight panic. *I need to eat—and soon!* If we interpret this as a hunger emergency, we are likely to approach food in unhealthy ways, consuming high-calorie snacks or fast foods with little nutritional value—anything to overcome this unpleasant feeling. But an exercise of *bare attention* opens another option. We simply abide in the experience: *This is only hunger; this is what hunger tastes like.* We are now less provoked by the automatic responses that lead, too often, to unhealthy eating.

We face a more daunting challenge in practicing bare attention with an emotion like anger. As this emotion arises, negative judgments seem to arise spontaneously. *I should not feel angry! Anger is sinful. If I were more generous or more mature or more forgiving, I would not be angry now.* The goal of bare attention is to simply abide with the emotion of anger itself. This often enables us to distinguish anger from the negative associations and harsh judgments that accompany our feelings. Once attended to, the negative associations that render anger toxic often fall away. Now we are left with the emotion itself—*What I am feeling is simply anger.* There is great freedom to be gained from such a shift. Epstein observes, "Instead of running from difficult emotions (or hanging on to enticing ones) the practitioner of bare attention becomes able to contain any reaction: making space for it, but not completely identifying with it."

Epstein links this exercise of mindfulness with the common experience of carrying unresolved feelings within ourselves. "If aspects of the person remain undigested—cut off, denied, projected, rejected, indulged, or otherwise unassimilated—they become the points around which the core forces of greed, hatred, and delusion attach themselves." The result is that we tense up around that which we are denying, and we experience ourselves through our tensions. This defensiveness has dire consequences. "When we refuse to acknowledge the presence of unwanted feelings, we are as bound to them as when we give ourselves over to them indignantly or self-righteously."

But Epstein adds a hopeful note: developing the mindfulness practice of bare attention changes the way we experience our emotions. When we recognize the fearful associations that complicate our emotional responses, we can experience our emotions more directly. We learn to be with our feelings in a new way. Acknowledging a threatening emotion removes some of its sting; becoming conscious of a strong feeling as it arises gives us more freedom in determining our response. Epstein concludes, "The paradox of bare attention, however, is that in this acceptance is a simultaneous letting go."

These practices of mindfulness help us become more present to our life, more attentive both to the turmoil within and the invitations to compassion toward others. Thus mindfulness deserves a privileged place in Christian spirituality.

Additional Resources

The virtue of self-love is explored by James Keenan in *Moral Wisdom* and by Julie Hanlon Rubio in *Family Ethics: Practices for Christians.* Also see Michael Lawler and Todd Salzman, "Virtue Ethics: Natural and Christian," in *Theological Studies.*

The quotation on spiritual exercises is from Aaron Stalnaker, *Overcoming Our Evil: Human Nature and Spiritual Exercises in Xunzi and Augustine.*

For discussions of mindfulness, see *The Mindful Way through Depression* by Mark Williams, John Teasdale, Zindel Segal, and Jon Kabat-Zinn. Jon Kabat-Zinn continues this discussion in *Coming to Our Senses: Healing Ourselves and the World through Mindfulness.*

Psychologist Daniel Siegel relates the wisdom of the body to mindfulness in his *Mindsight.* Thich Nhat Hanh and Lillian Cheung explore *Savor: Mindful Eating, Mindful Life.* For the discussion of the Buddhist practice of bare attention, see Mark Epstein, *Thoughts without a Thinker* and his *Open to Desire.*

The examination of consciousness presented here is adapted from *The Ignatian Workout: Daily Spiritual Exercises for a Healthy Faith.* See also Roger Haight's reflections on the spiritual exercises of Ignatius Loyola in *Christian Spirituality for Seekers.*

PART TWO
Sexuality and Justice

Chapter Six

Encounters of Sexuality and Justice

Justice in sexual ethics requires us to recognize, support, and promote the equality of the genders, with the understanding that such work still has much to accomplish.
—James Keenan

Sexuality embraces love, affection, intimacy. Justice focuses on obligation, law, and social order. Sexuality is about desire and thrives in our private lives; justice is about duty and monitors the public realm. At first glance these dynamics seem quite separate, but in fact they often intersect.

Sexuality's Link with Justice

"Sexuality is a passionate spark, deep within, that energizes us for justice-making as well as love-making." Moral theologian Marvin Ellison here insists that the force of erotic energy moves us toward others, both in affection (sexuality) and care (justice). To appreciate the full scope of this erotic power we will need to expand our vision of sexuality beyond genital activity. "Sexuality encompasses more than genital sex and, when understood comprehensively, expresses our embodied longing for intimacy and community. Erotic power is a precious gift we humans may use or misuse, often with tragic consequences for self, others, and the community itself." Our longing for a fruitful bonding with others motivates both sexual desire and the pursuit of justice. "In this light, the moral problematic is not sex or even strong eroticism, but rather the perversion of human desire by sexual injustice."

Sexuality is an essential dynamic in individual maturity, in interpersonal relationships, and in society as a whole. Sexual sharing with a beloved partner shapes and strengthens the mutual commitments of marriage. Here, sexuality and justice are linked in practices of respect, mutuality, and compassion. But sex is also recruited into the service of coercive and destructive behavior—from the *soft power* of sexual harassment and Internet pornography to the *hard power* of sexual domination and rape as a strategy of war. In these experiences of sexual constraint and violence—whether within or without marriage—sexuality loses its connections to both justice and love.

Contemporary moral theologians are attuned to ways in which social institutions can distort erotic power by fostering or shielding behaviors that are habitually unjust. Their intent is to identify ways in which society's norms and expectations—in marriage, in the workplace, in church structures—can witness to and support a love that is just. Margaret Farley describes, "[T]hese are claims to freedom from unjust harm, equal protection under the law, an equitable share in the goods and services available to others, and freedom of choice in their sexual lives—within the limits of not harming or infringing on the just claims of the concrete realities of others."

Ellison reminds us how intimately linked are our sensual connection with the world and our attentiveness to injustice. If we are out of touch with our own body and its sensual life, we are more likely to be unconcerned about the suffering of others. "By staying attuned to what feels right to us and by nurturing this awareness in the whole of our lives, we become less willing to tolerate abuse, injustice, and human cruelty. We become more and more desirous of living freely."

Ellison traces the ways that the erotic power of compassion—for oneself and others—engenders and defends just expressions of love. Since the term *erotic* is sometimes misunderstood, especially in religious discussion, Susan Ross's definition is especially valuable: "[T]he erotic is that creative energy which comes from deep within our being, which we have been taught to fear, but which fuels joy, relationships, and mutuality." In Ellison's understanding, erotic power supports personal identity, playfulness, and just relations. "The erotic can fuel our passion for justice.

It invites us to take ourselves seriously as sexual persons, playfully as erotic equals, and persistently as those who refuse to accept oppression as the way things must be."

The moral awareness that is the touchstone of justice is rooted in a sensual attunement to our world. Ellison continues:

> Moral knowing is rooted in feeling, and we depend upon sensuality to grasp and value the world. When sexuality is feared and evaded, people lack responsiveness and run the risk of becoming out of touch with what causes joy, suffering, and vulnerability, including their own. A people alienated from their bodies are more likely to be content with, and even at home with, pain and oppression.

Needs of the Spirit: Encounters of Justice and Sexuality

Both sexuality and justice are moral needs without which our lives will not flourish. Susan Neiman insists, "[W]e have moral needs, needs so strong they can override our instincts for self-preservation … they include the need to express reverence and the need to express outrage … the need to see our own lives as stories with meaning—meanings we impose on the world, a crucial source of human dignity—without which we hold our lives to be worthless." Michael Ignatieff argues that "humans do not merely have their needs; they seek to make them bearable by compassing them in meaning, in the language of providence, in the mythology of original sin"—and, we would add, in a morality of justice and sexuality.

But linking justice with human need raises other concerns. The Stoic tradition that has so influenced American life has seen needs as diminishing our human dignity. For the Stoics, Martha Nussbaum notes, "need itself does not have dignity … [the Stoics] do not think of the hunger of the body, its needs for shelter, for care in time of illness, and for love, as among the ingredients in its dignity." For many of us modern Stoics, needs exist as embarrassing reminders of our continuing vulnerability. To be *needy* seems to diminish us. Stoic virtue would demand that we transcend this vulnerability—or at least keep it out of public view. In American life today we see bracing examples of people and organizations caring for those in need, bringing into public view those whose wounds are often made worse by sexual injustice.

Margaret Farley's discussion of *just love* addresses both the affection we share in intimate relationships and the care we are meant to extend to the most vulnerable members of society. In the Tenderloin section of San Francisco, three ministries—during the day, in the early morning, and at night—are extending a hand to these marginalized members of society.

The Tenderloin is a triangular twenty-block neighborhood with twenty thousand inhabitants. These people are largely poor and are often homeless or marginally housed, and many suffer from problems of mental health, addiction, or both. After the 1906 earthquake, this section of San Francisco was developed to house the many immigrant workers in the city. Now nearly all its former apartment buildings have been converted into single-resident-occupancy (SRO) hotels—consisting of multiple narrow rooms, often minimally furnished, with common toilets and showers on each floor. The current population of the Tenderloin includes five distinguishable groups: elderly persons who have fallen on hard times, the mentally ill, those struggling with addiction, unemployed military veterans, and recent immigrants.

A Sanctuary of Sleep

For the thousands of people who live on the San Francisco streets, including those few who have access to sponsored nighttime shelters, sleep can be elusive. Many homeless persons force themselves to stay awake all night to avoid being attacked or robbed. Most SROs and sponsored shelters in the Tenderloin close in the early morning. Unless documented medical conditions require otherwise, even those fortunate enough to find shelter overnight must leave these buildings at that time. And the city's recent ban on sitting or lying on sidewalks means homeless people have to keep moving throughout the daylight hours.

So early each morning, scores of homeless people gather outside St. Boniface Church. This is a large Catholic church located in the heart of the Tenderloin neighborhood. Built by German immigrants over a century ago, the church has an active current parish membership that is quite small. In recent years, the church has implemented a ministry of welcome, opening its doors each morning between six o'clock and eleven o'clock as a safe haven for the homeless. "The ornately painted ceiling, stained-glass windows, huge marble columns, and organ pipes high above the wooden pews could make St. Boniface Church a stop on the tourist trek, but the loud snores and incense burned to help cover pungent smells quickly indicate this isn't your standard sanctuary." But the street people who wait to enter the spacious church do find sanctuary here, a safe place to stretch out and enjoy several hours of uninterrupted sleep. The clean restrooms that are available provide a bonus. Surely Saint Francis of Assisi, for whom this magnificent city is named, would be pleased with this arrangement.

Night Ministry

Night Ministry is a nationwide interdenominational initiative serving in many large metropolitan areas across the United States. This ministry has a strong presence in the Tenderloin neighborhood. As described in its mission statement,

> The San Francisco Night Ministry provides middle-of-the-night compassionate non-judgmental pastoral care, counseling, referral and crisis intervention to anyone in any kind of distress. Through our Crisis Telephone Line staffed by trained volunteer Crisis Line Counselors; and through person-to-person encounters with ordained clergy on the streets, this ministry is available every night of the year from 10:00 p.m.–4:00 a.m.

An ordained Lutheran pastor serves as lead minister in the Night Ministry serving the Tenderloin; he is joined by volunteers who are members of several local congregations. These trained volunteers—some with professional credentials in counseling and social services—walk the streets of distressed neighborhoods, offering a ministry of presence and crisis counseling. The Night Ministry also operates a nightly telephone crisis line. Periodically, *open cathedral* worship services are celebrated in available public settings where the homeless and others in need would feel welcome.

Care through Touch

Mary Ann Finch established the Care through Touch Institute thirty years ago as a massage-based ministry in Berkeley, California. Inspiration came from her previous experience providing massage in leprosariums in India. In its early years, the Berkeley-based program trained volunteers in massage therapy who would, in turn, provide care through touch to vulnerable members of society—homeless women and men, and veterans and others without jobs, as well as unmarried teenage mothers who needed help in learning to care for their infants. Some years later, Mary Ann moved her program to the destitute Tenderloin neighborhood in San Francisco. There she continues to train volunteers, who now provide therapeutic massage in twenty different locations, including both social service agencies and church facilities. People from the local area, primarily homeless women and men—often additionally burdened by mental illness or addiction—arrive and sign in for a twenty-minute neck-and-shoulder massage. Over the next three hours, the volunteers provide this ministry of caring touch to members of a population seldom experiencing such respectful physical care.

Mary Ann describes this ministry:

> Trained massage practitioners provide care through touch, and emotional and spiritual support, to the *untouchables* within our own communities—the homeless poor found in every segment of our society. We serve veterans of war, the cast-away elderly, people afflicted with threatening illnesses, addicted and seriously mental ill people, and women and children fleeing domestic violence.

Mary Ann traces the links between sensual care and a just society:

> Homeless and marginally housed people are rarely touched in a loving way. Without touch, many have become numb to their bodies. They have become invisible to themselves and to their communities. They have forgotten that they belong. Therefore, many had

66

stopped caring for themselves and their communities. Compassionate touch addresses these experiences of disconnect and alienation. It awakens people to their bodies and their surroundings. It empowers people to act in loving ways toward themselves and others.

Sexual Injustice

James Keenan, an influential theological voice, focuses on the challenge that sexual violence in society raises for Christian ethics. He insists that "this Catholic sense of justice calls us to recognize when others are denigrated ... by the commercialization of sex, from prostitution to the kidnapping and transport of minors." He identifies justice as the impulse that "moves us to enter into the chaos of those whose dignity is compromised by sexual inequities." Keenan acknowledges the work of sexual justice that remains to be done. "A justice informed by mercy looks to those who because of sexuality (histories of abuse, sexual dysfunction, orientation questions) cry out for protection, sanctuary, support and hospitality." Thus church leaders, when examining issues of sexual abuse, "will also need to review their role in the issue of justice and civil rights for gays and lesbians. Here church leaders have much work to do in learning about the experiences and self-understanding of these people, especially those who are devoted members of the Church including those in ministry."

Eroticizing Domination

Marvin Ellison's analysis of sexuality and power includes a challenging discussion of erotic domination—the linkage of sexual attraction and the impulse to control and constrain. In the animal kingdom, copulation and coercion seem to go together. Nature programs on PBS show the male lion wrestling the lioness to the ground in an exchange that unites force with sex. And men will sometimes admit that fantasies of domination at times figure in their own sexual arousal.

Domination and sexuality come together in what Ellison names *eroticism*. "Eroticism is about having someone under your control or feeling safe by being placed under another's power. Control is erotically charged, and compliance to authority titillating." In this setting, sex serves as "a control dynamic between a powerful subject and *his* submissive object. Unfortunately, traditional Christian sexual ethics is implicated in this mess because it, too, has perpetuated an ethic of male entitlement and male ownership of women and female bodies."

Margaret Farley adds her perspective: "Sexuality conditioned by male gender supremacy eroticizes power inequalities, bolsters male control, and increases people's comfort level with oppression." The clergy sexual abuse scandal in the Catholic Church has arisen, in part, due to the power inequalities that separate clergy from children and women. The US military is facing a similar crisis. Women in initial training are subject to male trainers who are also their superiors. When these women suffer sexual assault, they are expected to report this to their superiors—often the very persons who are abusing them. In both social settings—religion and military—power inequalities pave the way for sexual injustice.

A Justice Ethic for Sexuality

Margaret Farley approaches the détente of sexuality and justice from the side of justice. She insists that *just love* is rooted in "the kind of justice that everyone in the community or society is obligated to affirm for its members as sexual beings. Whether persons are single or married, gay or straight, bisexual or ambiguously gendered, they have claims to respect from the Christian community as well as the wider society." Marvin Ellison approaches this relationship from the side of sexuality, exploring how our sensual attunement to others influences our just attentiveness to them.

Farley acknowledges that the "advanced notions of justice in bonds between persons have not yet been fully translated into the sexual dimensions of personal relations." The equality of all citizens and their protection under the law, especially regarding their sexual experience or expression, has yet to be fully implemented. Farley's goal is "to refine a justice ethic for sexuality," though she admits that "the task of articulating such a framework (for recognizing power inequalities in gender relations) has barely begun."

Ellison names the challenge that a justice ethic of sexuality would face: "We must find creative ways to enter into, and not just talk about, genuine solidarity with women, gays, and people of all colors, and with survivors of sexual and domestic abuse, all of whom are rising up in resistance to erotic injustice in this culture."

Ellison concludes,

> Hope is literally embodied as our unquenchable passion for justice and as our refusal to dismiss any suffering as inconsequential. Our moral and spiritual commitment is to leave no one out and leave no one behind. Loving well, we are coming to understand, requires pursuing justice in all social relations, including those closest to our skin.

A Morality of Duty and an Ethic of Desire

Justice alerts us to commitments and obligations to which we are accountable. Sexual desire draws us toward relationships that can be life-giving. Our lives are shaped by both duties and desires. Both maturity and holiness lie in achieving a fruitful balance.

Christian discipleship challenges us in two imperatives: obligation ("Thou shalt not") and invitation ("Follow me!"). Theologians offer insight into the significance of this distinction—expanding our moral gaze beyond a narrow focus on what we must *avoid* to include a more comprehensive view of those ideals we can *pursue*. These complementary dynamics are often framed in terms of morality (the discussion of our obligations) and ethics (a consideration of human flourishing, the realm of aspirations and desires).

Morality—the traditional domain of justice—is rightly guided by the exercise of disciplined reason. Ethics—with its interest in human flourishing—finds resources in emotion and imagination as well. Charles Taylor argues that Christian reflection, by limiting its analyses to rational considerations of duty and obligation, has often been trapped "in the corral of morality." The contemporary challenge, as he describes it, is to broaden our ethical focus to include hopes and aspirations that move us toward human flourishing—the expansive well-being for which the Creator has designed all of humankind.

Morality trains our attention on universal laws and general moral codes, which help societies answer the basic question "What is the just response, required equally of all?" Ethics focuses on human flourishing, asking the question "What values are worthy to pursue, for the fuller realization of humanity's hopes?" When human flourishing comes into focus, the goal of avoiding evil is no longer sufficient. Maturity requires an ongoing dialogue between duty and desire. In this dialogue, duty plays a guardian role. Individual desires and personal hopes are often beset by self-deception. Thus a sense of moral obligation remains critical, Paul Ricoeur notes, "as a means of testing our illusions." The positive aim of the good life must be submitted to the test of moral obligation.

For Ricoeur, obligation and aspiration—rules and desire—must find a balance. Conscience matures and becomes trustworthy in the expectable tension of harmonizing our own voice with the other influential voices that dwell in our memory. We do not banish these formative sources from our conscience, nor do we merely submit to them. Instead, over a lifetime we *find our voice* by integrating these authoritative voices into a harmonious chorus of conscience that honors both our heritage and our individuality.

Additional Resources

Marvin Ellison explores links between sexuality and justice in "Reimagining Good Sex: The Eroticizing of Mutual Respect and Pleasure," in *Sexuality and the Sacred*. See pages 248–250. Also see his keynote address, "Reimaging Sexuality as Our Passion for Justice," delivered at the national conference at St. John's University, Collegeville, Minnesota, June 10, 1998.

Margaret Farley explores the links between sexuality and justice in *Just Love: A Framework for Christian Social Ethics*. See especially pages 177ff and 207ff.

Also see James Keenan's keynote speech, "Virtues, Chastity and Sexual Ethics," presented at the first Interfaith Sexual Trauma Institute conference at Collegeville, Minnesota, June 10, 1998.

Susan Neiman reflects on moral needs in *Moral Clarity*. See also Michael Ignatieff, *The Needs of Strangers*. Martha Nussbaum discusses the Stoic devaluation of need in *The Fragility of Goodness*.

In his encyclical letter *Deus Caritas Est* (God Is Love) Pope Benedict XVI discusses relationships among *eros*, sexuality, justice, and charity in Catholic theology and Christian life.

The description and quotations relating to the ministry for the homeless at St. Boniface Parish in the Tenderloin are drawn from Heather Knight's "Project Gubbio at St. Boniface: Sanctuary of Sleep," which appeared in *SFGate* (Monday, March 12, 2012). For more information about the Night Ministry, see (www.thenightministry.org) and for Care through Touch Institute, see (www.carethroughtouch.org).

For further discussion of the distinction between ethics and morality, see Paul Ricoeur, *Figuring the Sacred* and Charles Taylor, "Iris Murdoch and Moral Philosophy," in his *Dilemmas and Connections*.

Chapter Seven

Honoring the Disabled Body

> *We are all differently abled from one another ... The problem is to change how we assess the value of individuals and their lives, to reach for a more ecumenical take on healthy [and an] accommodation of difference rather than erasure of it.*   —Andrew Solomon

Nancy Eisland was born with a congenital bone disorder in her hip. She experienced her first surgical intervention at age seven, and by the time she was thirteen had undergone eleven operations. For most of her life, Nancy's mobility was enhanced by the use of a wheelchair. She married, and she and her husband, Terry, had one child. As a young adult, Nancy was drawn to Christianity and initially joined the Assembly of God Church. Soon after, her interest in ministry led to graduate studies at the Candler School of Theology. Early in her time at Candler, Nancy approached the academic dean with a serious complaint. She was concerned that the curriculum lacked any genuine consideration of faith or spirituality that reflected the experience of disabled persons. In that discussion, the dean presented a challenge—that Nancy herself bring this perspective into the theological and pastoral conversation. Taking up this task, Eisland began the research that formed the basis of her influential book *The Disabled God.*

The Language of Disability

The public discussion of physical and intellectual disability has been initiated by people who are themselves not disabled—or, as Eisland states, by those who are "temporarily-abled." She uses this term as a stark reminder that each of us stands vulnerable to the physical diminishments provoked by disease, accident, or simply the inevitable processes of aging. To the notion of "the temporarily-abled" we might add the term "apparently-abled" to include all of us who are more successful in hiding our woundedness. In *Far from the Tree*, his critically acclaimed examination of children with disabilities and their families, Andrew Solomon observes, "All kinds of attributes make one less able. Illiteracy and poverty are disabilities ... extreme age and extreme youth are both disabilities. The problem is to change how we assess the value of individuals and their lives, to reach for a more ecumenical take on *healthy*."

Eisland discusses the terminology that has developed to describe persons living with disabilities. The most widely used term has been *handicapped*—focusing on lack or deficiency and suggesting that those who are named here are to some degree defective or inadequate. And society usually pursues its response in terms of *rehabilitation*. Where disability is viewed as an economic problem, vocational rehabilitation becomes a goal. And programs are developed to provide employment counseling and job training. Where disability is seen as largely a medical problem, rehabilitation efforts lead to new medical specializations and to a wide range of direct services to support those living with disabilities.

These rehabilitation efforts continue to bring significant benefits to many persons living with physical and intellectual disabilities. But Eisland points to an underlying concern: too often the vocabulary of *handicapped* and *rehabilitation* interprets disability as a *problem of individuals* who are seen primarily as *recipients of care*. This perception casts those who are living with disabilities as needy individuals dependent on outside expertise, rather than as active participants who are themselves contributors to society. And many church-sponsored institutions have practiced a *segregational charity* that—in pursuit of health and safety—often removes those living with disabilities from regular participation in civic and even church life.

For Eisland, the major social transformation has been recognizing those living with disabilities as members of a social group ready—and able—to assume an active role in their progress toward full social participation. "The public goal now becomes *access* or *accessibility*—not just physical modifications of living space and public facilities."

Self-advocacy groups today insist on at least three levels of social response to those with disabilities: freedom from neglect, abuse and the violation of patients' rights; access to education and employment; and the opportunity to live an independent life. Andrew Solomon adds, "[T]he social model of disability demands that society modify the way business is done to empower people with disabilities, and we make such adjustments only when lawmakers accept that life can be painful for those who live at the margins."

A Theology of Disability

In the ancient world, people struggled to make sense of suffering. A first resolution was to connect suffering to moral fault. At the time that Hindus and Buddhists in India were exploring the concept of *karma* (our present suffering stems from wrongdoing in an earlier life), the people of Israel linked suffering with personal sin. Suffering—so publicly on display in physical disabilities, such as blindness and leprosy—must come to humans as moral punishment. The New Testament includes a reminder of this pervasive view, as Jesus is questioned about the origin of a man's blindness: "[H]is disciples asked him: 'Rabbi, who sinned, this man or his parents, that he was born blind?'" (John 9:2).

Another biblical vision of suffering and disability came to exercise great authority: in the book of Isaiah we read of a "suffering servant" who mysteriously bears the accumulated ills of his community. In moving poetic language we are told, "He was pierced for our transgressions, he was crushed for our iniquities; the punishment that brought us peace was upon him, and by his wounds we are healed" (Isaiah 53:5). A spirituality of scapegoat and sacred victimhood arose from this biblical memory. Christians saw in this "suffering servant" a prophecy of Jesus and his redemptive suffering. Here suffering is something to be borne; we are not called to challenge the injustice that is at the root of much distress, nor are we called to heal the suffering that can be relieved; suffering is simply to be endured. Christian piety sometimes suggested that suffering was to be welcomed, even sought, as a means to gain spiritual merit.

Blessed and Broken

A theology of the Incarnation honors the physical suffering of Jesus. It finds inspiration in the postresurrection accounts of Jesus appearing to his disciples, inviting them to touch his wounds. Here the risen Christ offers his wounded body as a sign of his living presence and as a guarantee of his identity. "In presenting his wounded body to his friends, the resurrected Jesus is revealed as a disabled God" (Eisland). And it is this Jesus Christ, our disabled God, whom we proclaim in faith to be sitting at the right hand of the Father.

In one interpretation of the biblical evidence, Jesus suffered so that we would not have to. Yet another interpretation seems more accurate: Jesus suffered to show us how to face the pain and losses that eventually disable us all. His suffering did not miraculously remove ours; instead, his suffering—even unto death—illumined a path for us to follow. In this spiritual vision, Jesus stands as icon of blessed and broken: suffering and disability not magically erased, but embraced and even transformed.

Christians hold sacred the icon of the cross where Jesus's battered body is lifted up. Even in the magnificent crucifixes of Byzantine art where the risen Jesus is glorified, his injuries and scars endure. The manifestation of Jesus's transcendent identity does not happen apart from his battered body, but in and through his wounds. These disfiguring scars are not made to vanish; his transformation is precisely in his broken body.

Eisland explores the significance of this Gospel perspective for those of us today who live with disabilities. The message is not that physical remedy should not be sought but that spiritual transformation should not be delayed. Disability is not a barrier to religious experience or spiritual growth. Becoming a follower of Christ, being welcomed as a contributing member in the community of faith, need not be put off until one is seen by other people as whole.

A Spirituality of Disability: Vulnerability and Integrity

Jacob is alone, and it is night. Suddenly he is set upon by an unknown force. Jacob wrestles with this mysterious power through the night; only at first light does it dawn on him that his opponent is, in fact, his God. At the end of this frightening encounter, Jacob is blessed—"for you have struggled with God and humans and have survived." But he carries this wound with him for the rest of his life, "limping because of his thigh" (Genesis 32).

The disciple Paul described his own chronic physical difficulty as "a thorn in the flesh." In prayer he asked God to remove this affliction. But God was content that Paul should bear this weakness, this deficiency. "My power is made perfect in infirmity" (1 Corinthians 12). For both Jacob in the Hebrew scriptures and Paul in the New Testament, spiritual integrity is linked with, even dependent upon, physical infirmity. In other religious traditions as well, the shaman's healing power is often associated with psychic distress or physical disability.

In a culture like ours, committed to personal autonomy and independence, reminders of vulnerability make us uncomfortable. Our cultural roots in Stoicism incite us to be self-sufficient; emphasis on God's invulnerability in our religious heritage leaves us suspicious of our own needs. Yet at the heart of our faith stands the scandal of the Incarnation: God's Son become flesh, made vulnerable in the endless ways so familiar to mortals. And this vulnerability bore bitter fruit in the passion and death of Jesus. What do we learn here? Perhaps our own vulnerability is to be honored. More than simply a sign of weakness, our vulnerability may even be virtuous.

A spirituality of disability invites us to acknowledge our enduring vulnerability. We recognize the difference between the illusory ideal of perfection and the lifelong challenge of integrity. We all aspire to a life that is complete, perfect, without blemish. The cosmetic industry today thrives on this ideal: elective surgery promises the elusive ideal of a svelte figure, unwrinkled face, firm muscles. Commercial advertising, with its unblemished models and muscular sports heroes, invites us to participate in this fantasy future. Even scripture can be twisted to this ambition: "Be ye perfect, even as your heavenly father is perfect" (Matthew 5:48). Yet our life experience teaches us that this is not to be. To be mortal is to court bruises, to put up with limitations, to recognize mistakes, to forgive failure.

Integrity involves the ongoing effort to acknowledge and embrace our disparate "selves." Gradually we become able to accept our brokenness as an enduring part of our identity. The presence and participation of those living with disabilities can bring all of us to a more authentic understanding of what bodily integrity means. Through prayerful reflection, we come to see Christ's wounds as part of his integrity. It is not by transcending the body, but by embracing and living in and through one's actual body, that those living with disabilities—in fact, all of us— find the experience of transcendence in our embrace of the disabled God.

Sexuality and Disability

Sexuality is central to our self-awareness and self-acceptance. But for many people living with disabilities—whether physical or intellectual— the experience of sexuality often remains conflicted. Few positive role models are available in the larger public world. If we look to advertising or popular culture, sex and romance seem to be available only to those with "perfect" bodies. Anyone who is old or overweight or sick or disabled seems to be excluded. And disabled persons—children, adolescents, and adults—are often treated as incapable of sexual behavior and uninterested in intimate relationships.

In fact, many persons living with disabling physical or intellectual conditions are married. Their marriages often include the blessings and responsibilities of raising children. Increasingly, legal protections and social services are available to offer support. And evidence shows high levels of well-being within these families.

Resources for sex education, appropriate to the differing intellectual and physical capacities of those with disabilities, are now widely available. In the United States, the Sexuality Information and Education Council has adopted this comprehensive statement: "SIECUS believes that individuals with physical, cognitive, or emotional disabilities have a right to education about sexuality, sexual health care, and opportunities for socializing and sexual expression." In support of these rights, SIECUS advocates that "healthcare workers and other caregivers must receive comprehensive sexuality education, as well as training in understanding and supporting sexual development, behavior, and related healthcare for individuals with disabilities." The statement concludes, "The policies and procedures of social agencies and healthcare delivery systems should ensure that services and benefits are provided to all persons without discrimination because of disability."

Increasingly, residential settings honor the need for privacy that supports deepening relationships and sexual expression. But barriers remain. Many persons with disabilities lack opportunities to initiate or receive positive touch. Disabled bodies are often touched—sometimes painfully—by therapists and other medical personnel. Persons with physical and intellectual disabilities are disproportionately victims of sexual and physical abuse—often at the hands of family members or other caregivers. But experiences of affectionate embrace, soothing massage, vigorous exercise, athletic participation—these are often limited or even denied to those with disabilities.

Theologian Elizabeth Stuart points to "a whole cluster of uncomfortable ethical issues surrounding sexuality and disability over which there is much disagreement among disabled persons themselves." Among the most controversial is the question of sexual surrogates or sexual attendants, persons who are specially trained to provide some expression of sexuality to disabled persons.

The recent award-winning film *The Sessions,* in which Helen Hunt plays the role of sexual attendant, has brought this discussion to a wider audience. The film is based on the essay "On Seeing a Sex Surrogate," written by Mark O'Brien. O'Brien, who had contracted polio in 1955 at age six, was a poet and journalist. A vocal advocate for the disabled, he published an autobiographical account, *How I Became a Human Being: A Disabled Man's Quest for Independence.*

In *The Sessions,* O'Brien is portrayed by John Hawkes. Now an adult, O'Brien is not completely paralyzed; he can experience physical feeling, but his muscles no longer support his mobility or even allow him to breathe on his own. Aware that he will be permanently confined to his artificial breathing device, he raises a question to the priest who is his spiritual confidant. Would God support O'Brien's decision to find a sexual surrogate, who could help him experience the sensual delight of erotic touch and perhaps even intercourse? The priest, portrayed in the film by William Macy, declares, "I think God would give you a pass on this." Not all counselors or pastors would concur with this advice. But the film raises an important moral question: What is permitted, what is owed, to a person who is deprived of access to so basic a human experience? The interaction between Hunt and Hawkes is delicately presented. The film is neither pornographic nor provocatively erotic. Hunt's character makes it clear that she is not a prostitute. She serves instead as a skilled therapist leading her physically disabled client toward a fuller experience of his body and its sensuality.

Many health personnel and other thoughtful advocates today—including persons who are themselves disabled—support this understanding of sexual surrogacy as a form of therapy, an option that should be made more generally available. In Canada, for example, the Sexuality and Access Project has sponsored community-wide discussions of factors influencing sexual health. Among the basic principles guiding the discussion is the conviction that people with disabilities "have a right to access and information and resources about their sexual health and [to] support in expressing their sexuality"—including access to the use of attendant services. In Holland, the Disabilities and Sexualities Group defends this practice. The group's founder, Pascale Ribes, insists that "sexual assistance is about allowing a disabled person who can't access sexuality in [a] satisfying way to reconnect with the body." Marcel Nuss, a disabled person who breathes with an artificial respirator, reinforces this view: "[S]ex helps the disabled to reincarnate themselves and recover their human respect."

Rituals of Healing

"I have experienced a laying on of hands that was restorative and redemptive," Eisland writes. "These physical mediations of God's grace have often kept me related to my body at times when all of my impulses pushed me toward dissociating from the pain-wracked, uncomfortable beast." Although the ritual laying on of hands is largely absent from the worship services of many denominations, Eisland urges that this consoling physical practice become an ordinary ritual of inclusion for people with disabilities.

Eisland recalls that

> as a child after spending several months in hospitals having my body rebuilt surgically, I was a participant in a powerful service of laying on of hands. In a charismatic meeting in a rural North Dakota parish, I experienced the body care of several elderly nuns schooled in physical attendance as nurses and touched by the spirit as

Christians. Their touch and tears were the body practices
of inclusion.

She found that in this simple reverent touching, "my body belonged in
the church. From that early age, I recall the physical sensation of having
my body redeemed for God as those spiritual women laid hands on me,
caressing my pain, lifting my isolation, and revealing my spiritual body."

For people with disabilities, such experiences of physical redemption
and ordinary inclusion are rare. Their bodies have too often been touched
by hands intent only on carrying out medical instructions or therapeutic
techniques. The attentive presence of caring touch helps both the giver
and the receiver connect with the body as a spiritual reality. As Eisland
testifies, "[S]uch experiences have transformative power."

Philosopher Martha Nussbaum writes of "healing without cure."
This dynamic is at play in embracing broken bodies and in forgiving
broken promises. Here healing does not erase our failures and overcome
all shortcomings. But these deficits are transformed into the honorable
wounds that mark our identity, defining who we are.

Andrew Solomon describes the practical shape of this healing: The
majority of parents of disabled children whom he interviewed appreciated
that "this has brought them closer to their spouses, other family members,
and friends; taught them what's important in life; increased their empathy
for others; engendered personal growth, and made them cherish their
child even more than if he or she had been born healthy." Another mother
wrote, "This thought [of her family's affection for the disabled child] runs
like a bright golden thread through the dark tapestry of our sorrow."

The work to create rituals of bodily inclusion is vital to the church
as a communion of struggle. The efforts to recover the hidden history of
people with disabilities and to restore their bodies within the church is
part of our conversion to the disabled God. Eisland concludes, "[B]reaking
the silence about their real lives as bodies makes possible a 'return to
the body'"—a positive body awareness that comes not from pursuing an
ideal but from accepting the reality that bodies evolve, become ill and
disabled, and die.

Christian churches must continue to assist temporarily able-bodied
persons as well as people with disabilities to appreciate that bodily
integrity calls for a lifelong spiritual and physical practice. Conversion

then involves learning to love what is carnal and our own lovely and limited bodies. Paul's reflections on the Christian community as "the body of Christ" include the counsel to offer special care for those members who are most vulnerable. "The members of the body that seem to be weaker are indispensable" (1 Corinthians 12:22). And he reminds us, "if one member suffers, all suffer together with it; if one member is honored, all rejoice together with it." Welcoming disabled members of the community to full participation, we "all rejoice together."

Additional Resources

Nancy Eisland's discussion appears in *The Disabled God: Toward a Liberating Theology of Disability*. Also see Elizabeth Stuart, "Disruptive Bodies: Disability, Embodiment and Sexuality," in *Sexuality and the Sacred: Sources of Theological Reflection*" and John Hull, "A Spirituality of Disability: The Christian Heritage as Both Problem and Potential," in *Studies in Christian Ethics*.

In *Far from the Tree*, Andrew Solomon explores parental and family responses to children born with disabilities—Down's syndrome, deafness, autism; see especially chapter 7. Mark O'Brien's autobiographical account, on which the film *The Sessions* is based, has been published as *How I Became a Human Being: A Disabled Man's Quest for Independence*. Martha Nussbaum discusses "healing without cure" in *The Fragility of Goodness*.

In *Marvelously Made: Gratefulness and the Body*, Mary Earle—a spiritual director herself living with a chronic disease—examines "the body as sacred text." For further reflection on the experience of disability, see *If I Had Wheels or Love: The Collected Poems of Vassar Miller* and *The Theological Voice of Wolf Wolfensberger*, edited by William Gaventa and David Coulter.

Chapter Eight

Sex and Power: Clergy Sexual Abuse

What began as a problem of personal misconduct ended as
a problem of hierarchical misuse of power and authority.
                                        —Joseph Chinnici

Sex and power intersect in many parts of life. Sexual sharing with a beloved partner is both erotic and powerful. But sex has also been recruited throughout human society for every kind of coercive and destructive behavior. The clergy sexual abuse scandal in the Catholic Church is a dramatic example of sex and power interacting in destructive ways. Here injustice and violence intersect, both in personal wrongdoing and in institutional malfeasance.

Historical Background

In *When Values Collide,* Joseph Chinnici offers a searing account of the current clergy sex scandal in the Catholic Church. He traces this crisis through five phases, beginning in the mid-twentieth century. Its initial phase (1950–82) was marked by "invisibility": the abusive behavior of a number of priests was seen as *sin,* a personal moral failing, a matter for private confession and repentance. There was no awareness of public accountability, no recognition of legal or criminal implications. The goal here was to maintain secrecy, in order to avoid scandalizing members in the faith community and to protect the religious institution from public disgrace. During the second phase (1982–88), a number of high-profile offenses came to public attention and "the disjunction between the cultural consensus about the intensity of the problem, the need for open disclosure, and the managerial reactions of the Church were becoming increasingly apparent to some in the society at large."

The third phase of this crisis (1988–94) saw a variety of institutional responses from the American and Canadian Catholic bishops. In 1992, Cardinal Bernardin initiated his influential proactive response in the Archdiocese of Chicago. That year also marked the tipping point in the Archdiocese of Boston: Here the ecclesial leader Cardinal Bernard Law was forced to retire, as the *Boston Globe* newspaper disclosed the pattern of neglect in the institutional management of the growing number of allegations. And in reaction against the lack of ecclesial integrity and absence of compassionate action toward victims and their families, the lay organization Voice of the Faithful was formed.

During the fourth phase (1994–2001), attention increasingly shifted from the malpractice of the abusers to failures of church leadership. "Ecclesiologically, the central cultural problem had ceased to be that of clerical sexual abuse and was fast becoming one of organizational incompetence and patterned institutional abuse of authority."

Chinnici describes the most recent phase, beginning in the year 2002. As victims of clerical abuse continued to come forward, lawsuits multiplied and several dioceses were forced to declare bankruptcy. During this period, "the hierarchy appeared frightened; the moral integrity of one's [leaders] seemed compromised; the help of experts, vague; the ordinary mechanisms of the civil and social order working for justice, inadequate." In their early responses to reports of clerical abuse, church leaders, seeking to guide the American Catholic community in a highly secular and Protestant-dominated environment, sought at all costs to avoid public scandal. But soon this policy of avoidance generated a yet larger scandal.

Chinnici concludes his careful analysis: "What began as a problem of personal misconduct ended as a problem of hierarchical misuse of power and authority." He judges that "the sexual abuse crisis involved not simply the complications of power ... but also the discovery of deeply embedded moral disorders that damaged the perceived identity of the Church, its public credibility as a teacher of truth, and its moral witness to holiness and justice."

Holy Church, Sinful Church

All sexual abuse is first and foremost an abuse of power. It
is an abuse of power in a sexual form ... Spiritual power
is arguably the most dangerous power of all.
—Bishop Geoffrey Robinson

Chinnici cites the current crisis as "a watershed in the history of American Catholicism." The appropriate response at this point is not simply a matter of identifying perpetrators, paying settlements, and returning to life as it was before. The deeper questions must be faced—questions about power relationships within the church, between laity and clergy, between women and men.

A number of scholars—theologians, canon lawyers, psychologists—have attempted to respond to the structural dysfunction that lies at the heart of this now worldwide scandal. Ethicist Lisa Sowle Cahill describes current church structures as "a closed society largely insulated from the realities and values of ordinary people and in denial of many aspects of human sexuality" (quoted by William Spohn, in *Sin Against Innocents,* p. 156). She points to the areas of needed reform: overcoming the church's cultural isolation and initiating a more positive embrace of sexuality.

Observing that "the canonical system has been an abysmal failure at dealing with clergy sexual abuse," canon lawyer Thomas Doyle locates the core difficulty in "the very nature of the Catholic Church governance." He explains: "There is no separation of powers, hence no checks and balances and no true accountability for Church leaders." As a result, "all power in ecclesiastical governance resides in individuals and not in collective bodies." Councils and conferences are merely advisory to the bishop who holds "the full juridical, legislative, and executive powers in his diocese."

This absence of accountability is evident in the functioning of the diocesan review boards mandated in the 2002 "Charter for the Protection of Children and Young Persons." In fact, local bishops are under no obligation to consult these boards; they may, at will, withhold from the board members information about particular offenders and pending charges. In defense of this dysfunctional arrangement, bishops have sometimes responded that "fraternal correction" is the more appropriate remedy to use in regard to offending clergy.

Christina Traina suggests that

> priestly pedophilia is ... a fitting symbol of our culture's
> failure to speak openly and honestly about proper uses
> of power, sensuality and desire. By forbidding the public
> evolution of a healthy, critical sensuality, the no-touch
> rules we put in place as protection against such violation
> likewise perpetuate, rather than remediate, our stunted
> ethic of eroticism.

Priests as Symbolic Persons

We are only now becoming aware of how parents and other authority figures exercise enormous symbolic power in the lives of children. Parents are often afforded an exalted status in the hearts of the young: they seem all-powerful, able to solve any problem and heal every wound. As the child matures, he or she will learn the painful but necessary lesson about the parents' fragility and humanity. This role of symbolic persons— parents, clergy, and psychological counselors being seen as bigger than life—entails what we might call a necessary distortion. This becomes a problem only if the parent, clergy, or counselor does not appreciate the psychological dynamics at play.

Priests function in Catholic life as symbolic persons. Commonly addressed as *Father*, the ordained leader exercises a parent-like authority in the community. The symbolic role of the clergy is intensified by the religious conviction that the priest stands in the faith community as representing both God and the church. This role grants him an elevated status deserving of great respect. But this esteem often serves to distance members of the clergy from the community of believers. The priest is to be revered—but from a distance. The isolation a priest may experience, being removed from other believers, may well lead to the kinds of inappropriate sexual contact so painfully prevalent in the church.

The status as symbolic representative of God makes members of the clergy especially admirable in the eyes of the young. Both a priest's official leadership role and his personal abilities will draw the attention of those in his care. Adults—but especially younger persons—are pleased to be in his company and flattered by his special attention. Complications develop when the priest is unaware of the special power that his role provides. A religious leader may not appreciate the extensive power that his function as ritual leader and pastoral authority in the parish (with the right to hire and fire) provides him.

Doyle judges that setting priests "apart, special, and above the lay people" undermines their accountability. He concludes, "[O]ne need look no further than rampant clericalism for an explanation of the fear, secrecy, and arrogance so prevalent in the clerical elite's inadequate response to the sexual abuse crisis."

Donna Markham and Samuel Mikail, in their research on the clergy sexual abuse scandal, point to three characteristics of offenders: "The prevalence of loneliness, the lack of rewarding close adult relationships, and the over-identification with the clerical role." If a priest is sexually immature, he may well have avoided any adult relationships that might demand genuine intimacy (an avoidance that seems to him to be supported by his celibate lifestyle). Instead, his work becomes his life. Ministry will likely place him in settings—in the confessional and in counseling situations—that introduce a kind of intimacy as grief-stricken or guilt-ridden parishioners bare their souls in the search for solace. These often intense experiences can be deceptive. While the priest receives intimate details of a person's life, he does not—should not—disclose himself at this level. Thus he exercises his ministry in a milieu of nonreciprocal intimacy.

In a period of exceptional stress in this all-consuming work, the priest may be tempted to search out some means of relief. Typical targets are food and alcohol, but sexual behavior may also beckon. This is unlikely to be with another adult (who is seen as too threatening), but with a child who is both charming and weak. Again, Markham and Mikail propose, "The child abuser frequently gravitates toward children in an effort to feel a sense of mastery and competence ... the abuser perceives the child 'partner' as socially and emotionally accepting and nonthreatening."

Eroticized Children and Sexual Violence

Ethicist Marvin Ellison has described the ways in which we eroticize— attribute erotic power to—a variety of relationships. For Ellison, eroticism is essentially a positive force that we can direct with wisdom and compassion. Yet problems arise when unequal exchanges and nonmutual relationships are eroticized. Then eroticism means having someone under your control; control becomes erotically charged, and compliance to another's control can become titillating.

Eroticizing power takes an extreme form in rape, but it functions also in marriages where coercion and domination are part of sexual practice. And, in the many cases of clergy sexual abuse, the adult has eroticized children.

Steven Rossetti, a priest and psychologist who has worked with priests for many years at the St. Luke Institute in Maryland, reflects on the destruction of trust in an abusive relationship.

> Research suggests that the most traumatizing element of sexual abuse for children is not the fact of their being used as a sexual object. Rather, the most damaging element is the abuse of human trust and thus, the abuse of power. The child was in a vulnerable position, i.e. the adult was given power over the child. This power was to be used for the child's good. Instead, it was abused.

The child who is sexually abused is unable to integrate two conflicting messages. The child sees the priest as a symbolic person—representing God's protective love and concern. The expectation implicit here is *all will be well*. But consider these examples: a thirteen-year-old girl who is a patient in a hospital is molested by the visiting priest chaplain who then brings her Communion the next morning; a fifteen-year-old boy is molested by the priest who also serves as his confessor. This abusive experience shatters the child's previous positive expectations. Research shows that, faced with this confusion, young people are most likely to blame themselves, deciding *this must be my fault*.

Spiritual Harm of Sexual Abuse

Bishop Goeffrey Robinson spearheaded an effective response to allegations of clergy sexual abuse in Australia. While acknowledging the many detrimental effects of such abuse, he judges that spiritual harm is "the first to occur and the last to be healed." He describes the devastating effects: "This is, I believe, the major spiritual harm caused by sexual abuse, the destruction of a delicate and elaborate system of meaning … the relationship is broken between sexuality and love, between trust and love, and between meaning and love."

In *Conversations with My Molester: A Journey of Faith*, playwright Michael Mack dramatizes the abuse he suffered at age eleven at the hands of his parish priest. Mack describes his initial delight in experiencing special affection from this religious leader. After being abused, he found that "simultaneous feelings of attraction and revulsion … persist in memory." Mack found himself "powerfully attracted, and powerfully repelled, finding self-loathing its own dismal ecstasy." Even now, Mack reports, he returns often to the continuing challenge: "One of the things that's difficult is to know how to forgive yourself for taking pleasure in that awful experience."

Psychologist Daniel Siegel describes the fragmented state of mind that can result from such trauma.

> A terrified child is faced with a biological paradox. Her survival circuits are screaming, "Get away from the source of terror, you are in danger!" But her attachment circuits are crying out, "Go toward your attachment figure for safety and soothing!" When the same person is simultaneously activating the brain's "go away" and "go toward" messages, it is fear without resolution—an unsolvable situation.

A New Ethical Space and Practice

Authoritative voices within the church have addressed the need for substantial change. Chinnici describes his hope for healing and renewal in the church's response.

> The challenge of the sexual abuse scandal as an abuse of power and as paradigmatic of the struggle between the hierarchical and communal structures of our social and ecclesial life demands the creation of a "new ethical space and practice" for relationships within the Church and between the Church and the world.

He envisions organizational structures that will "demand both an asceticism of humility, obedience, and dispossession and a focused commitment to establish trust." This new ethical space will permit a reevaluation of the sacred power of the priest and the restriction of the Sacrament of Orders to unmarried men. The education of clergy will be restructured to include a richer appreciation of sexuality. Acknowledging that these reforms may be seen by many current church leaders as threatening, Chinnici nevertheless insists on their necessity for the good of the whole church. "If we are to heal our society before it creates a climate that spawns the sexual abuse of children, we must heal our own broken sense of power and our grasping for control in violent and abusive ways."

Bishop Robinson, too, has advocated sweeping reforms to bring greater accountability to church structures. In evocative images, the Australian prelate indicts the institution: "I believe the Catholic Church is in a prison ... the prison of not being able to be wrong." He adds, "This need to be right at all times and in all matters, or at least to seem to be right, has been a major cause of the poor response to abuse within the church ..." Robinson's suggestions range from reform of the Curia (the bishops who staff the Vatican and exercise near total control over all governance) to the local election of bishops.

In one of his earliest actions upon assuming the responsibility as international leader of the Roman Catholic Church, Pope Francis established a twelve-person panel—consisting of six women and six members of the clergy—to address the urgent problems surrounding the sexual abuse of children by priests. This decision has renewed the confidence of many, both within the Catholic Church and beyond.

Additional Resources

Joseph Chinnici's discussion appears in *When Values Collide: The Catholic Church, Sexual Abuse, and the Challenges of Leadership.* For further analysis, see Steven Rossetti's *A Tragic Grace: The Catholic Church and Child Sexual Abuse* and Goeffrey Robinson's *Confronting Power and Sex in the Catholic Church.*

Sin against Innocents, edited by Thomas Plante, includes papers delivered at the 2003 conference on clerical sexual abuse convened at

Santa Clara University. Especially valuable essays there include Thomas Doyle, "Canon Law and the Clergy Sex Abuse: The Failure from Above"; Donna Markham and Samuel Mikail, "Perpetrators of Clergy Abuse of Minors: Insights from Attachment Theory"; and William Spohn, "Episcopal Responsibility for the Sexual Abuse Crisis." See also Linda Hogan's "The Clerical Sexual Abuse Crisis: Ireland and Beyond," in *Theological Studies*.

Marvin Ellison's address "Ethical Eroticism as a Call to Love Fearlessly: Re-imagining Sexuality as Our Passion for Justice" was delivered at the first national conference of the Interfaith Sexual Trauma Institute, on June 10, 1998. Katherine Seelve reviews Michael Mack's dramatic presentation in "Private Pain, Played Out on Public Stage" in the *New York Times* (Monday, January 14, 2013).

We examine the issue of religious power in "The Symbolic Role of the Leader" (chapter 11 in *The Promise of Partnership*) and in several chapters in *Leadership Ministry in Community*.

Chapter Nine

Marriage Equality: Reframing Lives of Committed Love

> *Our journey is not complete until our gay brothers and sisters are treated like everyone else under the law—for if we are really created equal, then surely the love we commit to one another must be equal as well.*
>
> —President Obama's Inaugural Address,
> January 21, 2013

"Fifty years ago, every state criminalized homosexual sex, and even the American Civil Liberties Union did not object." Offering this reminder, Michael Klarman notes the recent social dynamics that have accompanied the growing acceptance of marriage equality in the United States. In 1986, only 25 percent of Americans claimed to know a gay person; by 2001, 74 percent of Americans said they knew a gay person. The number of Fortune 500 companies offering benefits for same-gender couples rose from zero in 1990 to 263 in 2006.

These events, clustered together, mark an extraordinary change in the public acceptance of the right of same-gender couples to marry. In previous years, the civic debate about the legitimacy of same-gender relations often centered on personal freedom—the right of all citizens to behave as they choose in their own bedrooms. With the focus on individuals and the right to privacy, the argument was *leave us alone*. But *equality* is even more central to the American psyche than is *privacy*.

Thus, with the debate over "marriage equality," the focus has changed. Now the discussion centers less on the morality of personal behavior and more on the legal and economic rights available to all citizens. The plea moves from *leave us alone* to *include us* in the privileges and benefits of marriage. The moral high ground has shifted. At stake here is the opportunity available to all citizens to form legally recognized bonds of committed love. In every enduring marriage, whatever the gender composition, several vital signs will be evident.

Vital Signs of Marriage: Pleasure, Complementarity, Fruitfulness

The role of sexual pleasure in marriage has long been a stumbling block for the institutional church. The apostle Paul, himself unmarried, gave evidence of his concern: "[I]t is a good thing for a man not to touch a woman. But since sex is always a danger, let each man have his own wife and each woman her own husband" (Romans 7:1). Marriage is seen here as a means of harnessing unruly sexual desire. "If they cannot control their sexual urges, they should get married, since it is better to be married than be tortured." In this early season of Christian life, Paul viewed marriage as a concession to fallen nature, a regrettable necessity for most people. Several centuries later, Augustine expressed his own concern with sexual arousal and its threat to self-control. Burdened by the guilt and anxiety that clouded his own decade-long sexual relationship, he crafted his influential definition of marriage as "a remedy for concupiscence."

The challenge for the Catholic Church today is to recognize the sexual union shared by a committed couple as a good in itself; their mutual pleasure is fruitful quite apart from procreation. Catholic married couples have long experienced this blessing, but the institutional church has yet to fully appreciate this truth. Ironically, it was a non-Christian author writing at the very time that the Gospels were being crafted who spoke most eloquently of the broader fruitfulness of sex in marriage. Writing in the same language (Greek) and the cultural milieu of the New Testament, Plutarch described the blessings that arise from the sexual pleasure shared by a committed couple. Their mutual delight engenders a richer love; the pleasure itself supports love that will flourish.

In his words, Plutarch recognized that the couple's shared sexual pleasure (*hedone* in Greek) "causes to bloom" four virtues or goods of marriage. "Physical pleasure with a spouse is the seed of friendship and the participation in great mysteries. Though the physical pleasure is brief, from it grows day by day respect and grace, affection and faithfulness."

Perhaps not surprisingly, these virtues are also recommended throughout the New Testament—often in the context of marriage. Plutarch's initial virtue—*respect*—appears in the First Letter of Peter, where husbands are exhorted to respect their wives. In the Letter to the Hebrews, the writer insists that Christians should "hold marriage in great respect." Plutarch identifies the second virtue generated in the couples' shared sexual pleasure as affection—*agapesis;* in New Testament Greek this is the generous love of *agape,* the foundation of genuine friendship. For Plutarch, *faithfulness* is a third virtue that blossoms from shared sexual delight. In the New Testament, faithfulness points most often to the believer's adherence to God, but this fidelity is mirrored in a couple's enduring commitment to one another. Thus James Cotter, an Anglican theologian, writes of "those finer vibrations of pleasure that come from the complete trust that two people have in each other when they are faithful over a long period of time."

The fourth virtue in Plutarch's list comes closest to the heart of the Gospel's good news. Plutarch insists that shared sexual pleasure engenders in faithful lovers a *charis*—an expression of grace. This gracefulness—the distinctive style of shared life that a couple develops over time together—is rooted in shared sexual pleasure. Renowned church historian Peter Brown describes this grace of marriage as "the indefinable quality of mutual trust and affection gained through the pleasure of the bed itself ..." Shared sexual delight engenders not only children but a fuller love between the two partners. Pleasure itself is central in this blooming of married love.

Both in Plutarch and in the New Testament, charis includes another explicitly erotic nuance. The verb *charizesthai* means to gratify, to pleasure another in a way that evokes gratitude. Many couples today, whatever their sexual orientation, share Plutarch's conviction that making love can be a holy exercise in gratification: pleasuring one another in a way that is not mutual narcissism, but instead leads the partners to give thanks—to one another and to God, the source of all grace.

Complementarity in Love

As a marriage matures, each couple develops a style of interaction and mutual support that we speak of as a *complementarity*. This partnership is shaped by the gifts and needs that each individual brings to the relationship. In earlier generations, Christians were instructed in a hierarchical and gender-based complementarity. At the liturgy they heard, "Wives, be subject to your husbands, as is fitting in the Lord" (Colossians 3:18). In marriage preparation classes, the woman may have been instructed in "the primacy of the husband with regard to the wife and children, the ready subjection of the wife and her willing obedience," and warned against seeking "a false liberty and unnatural equality with the husband" (see Pope Pius XI's 1930 letter on marriage, *Casti Connubii*). In the past, marriages often came with such inbuilt expectations about the kind of cooperation and mutuality a couple might expect of one another.

More recently, Pope John Paul II sought to combine the modern vision of the equal dignity of each person in marriage with a traditional gender-based complementarity. Women, he was convinced, were created with a special genius for nurturance and compassion; this was to be their singular contribution to the couple's complementarity. If a wife engages in work beyond the family, such work should not be at "the expense of their true feminine humanity" (see the pope's letter, *Familiaris Consortio*, #23).

But as Traina testifies and many couples confirm, the fit and misfit of the couple's strengths and weakness "bear almost no relationship to our biological sexes." Describing the evolving relationship of herself and her husband, Traina continues: "[M]y sense of us as 'man' and 'woman' in magnetic attraction, strongly and exotically present when we met in our teens, has given way to my sense simply of two people in erotic partnership."

Catholic psychologist Sidney Callahan looks back at her own marriage:

> Those who have been long married and raised children of different genders can also question the rigid gender differentiations espoused in official Church teaching. They find that marital partners and children are shaped more by their individual differences, especially differences of character, than by gender differences.

The ideal of a strict equality in the marriage soon meets the reality of individuals with different vulnerabilities and talents. Most couples learn quickly that to demand such equality is folly; carefully measuring our mutual contributions ends as trying to "get even"—and the disaster that quickly ensues. A vital partnership confronts the expectations we have brought with us, most often unknowingly, to this common enterprise, and it entails forging and then renegotiating the values that will guide this partnership and family into the future. The traditional virtue of obedience—the wife obeying the husband—must be recrafted into a common discernment of how we will spend our resources, especially time and money. Couples in same-gender marriages attest that these challenges are also part of the complementarity that is a vital sign of their faithful unions.

From Procreation to Fruitfulness

The special dynamic of love is its desire to make more of itself. "Making love," we make more life—between us and beyond us. When our love generates new life in children, we are astonished and grateful. This is more than our doing! At first we may identify this new life as a "reproduction"—a new version of us. But parents quickly learn the mellow lesson of fruitfulness: our child is in fact unique—different from us, a separate person with new dreams and yet-unheard-of plans.

Most partners approach their marriage with hopes to be fruitful: to have something come of their love, to leave a mark, to make a contribution. For many centuries, fruitfulness was understood simply as biological fecundity. To be fruitful meant to have many children. Yet we are aware of married couples with many offspring whose lives seem pinched and ungenerous. And we know childless couples who contribute greatly to the larger community through actions of care and compassion.

The church has long taught that two key aspects of Christian marriage—the unitive force of mutual affection and the procreative welcome of children—are inseparable. The church struggles today to enlarge its vision of a marriage's fruitfulness. In the US Catholic bishops' recent (2009) letter on marriage, they acknowledge that couples who are beyond childbearing years "should continue to be life-affirming." They can do this by caring for the next generation, most especially their grandchildren. "They can also be nurturing through the exercise of care for those who are needy, disabled, or pushed to the margins of society, and by their support for or participation in works of charity and justice." This recognition of marital fruitfulness extending well beyond childbearing has yet to be applied to all the interactions of couples throughout their marriage, whatever their biological fertility.

Christina Traina notes that for Pope John Paul II, "only the act of unprotected intercourse ... symbolizes the total self-gift of spouses, who must always pursue mutual ecstasy accepting the possibility that it may result in a new child." But for Traina—and very many Christian couples— "generous, unprotected intercourse does not seem to me to be an absolute good." In marriage a variety of goods complements and influences the good of procreation. Many of these, including psychological and economic well-being, at times outweigh the good of procreation.

Writing from the experience of her own marriage, Traina comments, "Sex can be genuinely mutual, loving, just, fun, good, and even holy without having any procreative intent or being referred even remotely to procreation." She and her husband had delighted in sexual intercourse when they eagerly sought to become pregnant with each of their three children. But she notes that this was the case on perhaps ten occasions in their long marriage. At other times their lovemaking was intentionally nonprocreative, as it celebrated and reaffirmed the delight and fidelity of their committed love. Such testimony by a married moral theologian about her own marriage is, of course, utterly new in Catholic history.

Traina adds, "love-making is only rarely with intent for procreation. The rest of the time it serves as a symbolic statement and reinforcement of the couple's mutual love." She recalls the evidence from the Bible itself:

> Finally, the developing tradition's emphasis on marital union in sexuality, *The Song of Songs*, and the mystical tradition all celebrate mutual desire and its generous, loving, playful fulfillment as a good in itself. It is appropriate to continue to ask whether non-procreative forms of sexual delight are not perfectly appropriate within committed unions.

The evidence from married lives is that the fruitfulness of committed love is not confined to biological procreation. Fruitfulness takes many forms. To insist on procreation as the only fruit of marriage, Margaret Farley insists, represents "either a failure of imagination or a narrowness of experience that disallows an appreciation of all the ways in which humans bring life into the world." Fruitfulness, expanding well beyond the biological, "is both an obligation and an appeal, a requirement and a graced opportunity."

Sexual sharing that reinforces the continuing enhancement of the bonds of faithful love describes the lives of same-gender couples as well as heterosexual marriages. To describe the love of a homosexual couple as essentially "disordered" (as official Catholic documents have consistently done) is misguided and harmful. All humans are ordered toward life in abundance (John 10:10). For many of us, our own flourishing will include the care and nurturance of our children. For some of us, whether gay or straight, this will not be the case. Yet flourishing remains the goal. And for most of us, sexual sharing will be part of our flourishing.

Marriage Equality and "A School of Love"

Theologian Wendy Wright has explored the meaning of marriage as "a school of love." Every enduring union, whether of a heterosexual or a homosexual couple, becomes a site of ongoing development and discipline. The chief educational tools are the "busyness, caretaking, the noise and stuff of daily life …"

Dominican theologian Gareth Moore makes a compelling case for welcoming lesbian and gay couples to this formative experience, rather than simply denying or excluding their presence. He comments that "sincere, committed Catholics enter into [same-sex unions], in full knowledge that the Church—which they love and as a member of which they worship their Creator—condemns them for it." Moore offers several considerations to support the church's recognition of these unions.

> The first is the very lovelessness of much of the gay world, of which Christian traditionalists rightly complain. Given that homosexuals are in fact going to form sexual relationships, it is surely sensible to encourage them to form stable and loving same-sex relationships rather than enter into relationships which are unstable, even

fleeting, devoid of real love, and so contrary to their real happiness.

Moore continues his argument: "From a more theological point of view, we are all made for love. It is possible to love as a celibate, but for most people positive celibacy is not a realistic option; we are by no means all made for celibacy." He then turns to his main theme: "Traditional Catholic marriage has been a school for the self-giving love to which all are called." And, of course, "homosexuals too need a school of love ... a public, binding and permanent commitment to love each other in good times and in bad would help them to practice real love just as it helps heterosexual couples."

A school of love serves as more than private consolation. "Such a recognition would give homosexuals, particularly young ones, a positive public signal ... Entering into a publicly recognized gay civil union would give the partners certain legal rights and obligations," Moore continues, "and it would assure them that they are capable of faithful and generous love and that their love is worthy of being declared and celebrated publicly."

Moral theologian Stephen Pope argues that "same-sex marriage would encourage fidelity, increase monogamy and reward loyalty, self-discipline, stability, and reciprocal emotional investment." Ethicist Jean Porter argues "that one's sexual orientation so profoundly touches a person's identity that were one denied the ability to union in faithful and self-giving love, one would be denied what the Church holds to be intrinsic to the notion of human flourishing in the vast majority of human lives."

Conclusion

In the first decade of the twenty-first century, married theologians have entered with a new confidence and authority into the exploration of the dynamics of committed love. Moral theologians such as Christina Traina, both versed in the Christian tradition and comfortable with their own lived experience of marriage, published frank and persuasive essays on the roles of procreation and nonprocreative sex in Christian marriage. "Evidence about wholesomeness, balance and longevity in committed homosexual relationships must be attended to," Traina insists. She adds, "[H]onesty requires us to ask what it is about committed homosexual relationships ... that permits them to be stable and faithful, even without procreativity." Such discussions make clear that same-gender unions share the dynamics of affection, compromise, and mutual forgiveness that describe heterosexual marriage.

"The renewal of Christian sexual ethics," as Marvin Ellison observes, "requires greater candor about the widening gap between official church teaching about sex and the actual lives of most people." After noting that the Catholic Church "offers a profound core of moral wisdom regarding sex, marriage and the family that is badly needed," Stephen Pope sadly observes, "but the content and tone of its own statements have exacerbated matters by reinforcing the view of some observers that its sexual ethics is simply out of touch with contemporary experience."

Flourishing—"a human person fully alive" (St. Irenaeus)—does not arise in isolation; our lives flourish and become generous in the fragile unions of committed love. So gays and lesbians, too, must be welcomed to the feast and the lifelong discipline that is Christian marriage.

Additional Resources

Michael Klarman offers a helpful overview of shifting perceptions of gay and lesbian persons in the United States during the past half century; see *From the Closet to the Altar: Courts, Backlash and the Struggle for Same-Sex Marriage.*

Christina Traina contributes valuable insights in "Papal Ideals, Marital Realities: One View from the Ground," in *Sexual Diversity and Catholicism: Toward the Development of Moral Theology.* See especially pages 275 and 281–283. Also see her essay, "Under Pressure: Sexual Discipleship in the Real World," in *Sexuality and the Catholic Church.*

In *Body and Society: Men, Women and Sexual Renunciation in Early Christianity,* Peter Brown discusses Plutarch's *charis* of marriage in the context of Clement of Alexandria's understanding of passion and sexuality. Plutarch's essay "Dialogue on Love" is available in *On Love, the Family, and the Good Life: Selected Essays of Plutarch.* Jim Cotter's remarks on the pleasures of the long married appear in his essay "Homosexual and Holy" in *The Way.*

For official Catholic Church statements regarding marriage, see Pope Pius XI's 1930 encyclical letter, "Chaste Marriage Partners [*Casti Connubii*], and *Marriage: Love and Life in the Divine Plan,* a pastoral letter of the United States Conference of Catholic Bishops (2009).

Also see the volume of collected essays *Marriage in the Catholic Tradition: Scripture, Tradition, and Experience.*

Michael Lawler explores "Becoming Married in the Catholic Church: A Traditional Post-Modern Proposal," in *Intams Journal.*

Wendy Wright's discussion of "Marriage as a 'School of Love'" was given at a colloquium of social scientists and theologians on the theme of "Promoting and Sustaining Marriage as a Community of Life and Love," October 24–25, 2005. See also Gareth Moore, O. P. discussion in "Christians and Same-Sex Unions," *Intams Journal.*

Sidney Callahan's reflection on marital complementarity is available in her essay "Homosexuality, Moral Theology, and Scientific Evidence," in *Sexuality, Diversity and Catholicism: Toward the Development of Moral Theology.*

Stephen Pope examines "The Magisterium's Arguments against 'Same-Sex Marriage': An Ethical Analysis and Critique," in *Theological Studies.* James Keenan contributes to "The Open Debate: Moral Theology and the Lives of Gay and Lesbian Persons," in *Theological Studies.*

Chapter Ten

The Future of Our Religious Past

*Late have I loved you, Beauty so old and so new. Late have
I loved you.* —St. Augustine's *Confessions*

The early twentieth century brought with it extensive research in biblical, historical, and liturgical areas of the church's life. This research awakened Christians to an extraordinary variety and fluidity in their belief—a pluralism that had been long forgotten, all but erased by the prevailing myth of an unchanging, monochromatic belief system. Today we are more aware of what philosopher Charles Taylor has called "the future of our religious past ... which is now available for us to retrieve." The rich resources of our past are being remembered and made newly available to us—to appreciate, to question, and to reclaim as our own.

Reviewing the centuries-long development of Christian spirituality, we rediscover a decisive moment early in the theological tradition. This turning point has largely been overlooked, even forgotten for many centuries. But its significant influence continues.

A Moment in Time: The Year 391

The moment arrived as the fourth century was coming to an end. "In 391 CE the emperor Theodosius banned all public religious sacrifice and with it effectively shut down the religious competition to Christianity." From this time forward Christianity would be the uncontested religion

103

in Europe. That year stands as a landmark in the establishment of Christendom.

On this date, two great theologians, on either side of the Mediterranean, were developing very different approaches to Christian spirituality. Gregory of Nyssa (335–94) was the married bishop of a small diocese in eastern Turkey, a member of an illustrious family. His brother Basil was himself a bishop and theologian; his sister, Macrina, oversaw a family estate, and the community of Christians gathered there. In the year 391, Gregory initiated his commentary on the *Song of Songs*, a biblical text that celebrates Eros as the desire that leads the soul back to its Creator.

This same year, Augustine of Hippo (354–430) began his life as a priest; he was soon to be consecrated as a bishop in North Africa. Augustine was twenty years younger than Gregory and would outlive him by many decades. Augustine died in 430 at the age of seventy-five, leaving his autobiographical *Confessions* as a spiritual legacy. His vision of the Christian life would become the dominant view throughout Western Christianity for many centuries.

After the Great Schism in 1052 when the Western and Eastern Churches split over political differences, Gregory's optimistic vision was all but lost to Christians in the West. Scholars today are intent on reclaiming Gregory's spiritual optimism, as part of "the future of our religious past."

Four theological themes illustrate the differences that have developed within Christian spirituality East and West. First, if humanity is both *made in the image of God* and *born in original sin,* which belief takes priority? Second, what roles do desire, passion, and pleasure play in Christian life? Third, what does Christian conversion involve? And finally, who shall be saved?

Made in the Image of God

The conviction that humans are made in the image of God, dramatically expressed in the biblical account of the Creation, stood at the center of Gregory's optimistic spirituality. For Gregory all persons, not just Christians, bear this indelible image in their hearts. In fact, being created in the image of God is the overwhelming reality of human life. In Gregory's understanding, *image of God* is more than a pious metaphor.

It is a dynamic reflection of God's own goodness and beauty that lies at the core of every human. And this vital image arouses in the human heart an endless desire to draw closer to the Source of all goodness and beauty. This lifelong movement toward God is driven by the eros of desire.

In Gregory's view, our being created in the image of God outweighs the effects of original sin ... or *ancestral* sin, as it is more often identified in the Eastern Church. And for Gregory, original sin was not tightly bound to sexuality, as it would be for Augustine. Gregory acknowledged the rampant destructiveness of sin in the world. And Gregory was well aware of the mayhem that the passions, if not cultivated and shaped by Christian discipline, could cause. Forecasting the direction of thought in the Eastern Church, Gregory judged that this ancestral sin left all humans with the consequences of this sin but without the personal guilt. As a result, Gregory described humankind as born in grace. In his confident spirituality, Gregory celebrated the positive image of God embedded deep in the creature's heart as ultimately triumphant over the effects of sin. In the final analysis, Gregory believed in "the restoration of the divine image through the transformation of the passions" (J. Warren Smith).

Original Sin

For Augustine, original sin was so universally devastating that it trumped the original grace of being made in the image of God. Augustine was convinced that human nature was so injured by the original sin of Adam and Eve that our human nature could no longer be an active, trustworthy participant in our salvation. All human senses had been rendered unreliable. The many impulses and yearnings of the human spirit all led away from God toward an idolatrous attachment to creatures. Self-deception was now human nature's default position. Augustine famously observed, "Any good I do comes from God; any evil I do comes from me."

This first sin had badly distorted the image of God implanted in the human soul. Adam and Eve had been created in grace; all their offspring were born in sin. Because humans are born through sexual intercourse, sex itself became a guilty coconspirator in the transmission of sin to all generations. Augustine's own struggle with sexuality—which he so freely and repeatedly describes in his many writings—gave shape to this theology of sin and the ever-present perils of lust.

Sexual arousal for Augustine—and for all mankind, he assumed—clouded rational control, causing an intense sense of shame. Control and shame dominated Augustine's life and led to his pessimistic vision of humanity. As a Christian and a convert from Manicheanism, he believed that God had ordained procreation as a good. The puzzle for Augustine was how this good—generating children and ensuring the continuity of the species—could coexist with the loss of control and the intense pleasure that accompanied sexual intercourse. His own experience of sex, in his decade-long relationship with his unnamed partner, had always felt lustful, lacking in self-control, and therefore sinful. His tortured solution was that God allowed the evil of sexual pleasure for the sake of the good of marriage and children. From this belief sprang the long-held teaching of the Catholic Church that marriage is "a remedy for concupiscence."

A Life Shrouded by Shame

Confessions shows us, by the author's own admission, a person afflicted with a powerful sense of shame. Augustine tells us that he was ashamed of his youthful thefts, embarrassed by his grief and tears, and especially shamed by his uncontrollable sexual impulses. Late in his life, in *The City of God*, he explicitly acknowledged this trouble: "Now the soul is ashamed that the body, which is by nature inferior and subject to it, should resist its authority" (14:23), and he goes to great lengths to explain the shame that Adam and Eve felt in their nakedness after they had sinned. (See, for instance, 14:17.)

Theologian Margaret Miles traces this overwhelming sense of shame to his addictive personality. She argues that "Augustine felt himself to be what twentieth-century people might call a sex addict." Augustine confessed that "the habit of satisfying an insatiable appetite grievously tormented me" (*Confessions*, 6:12). For Augustine, sex was experienced as consuming and obsessive. As an addict, he found it impossible to enjoy a sexual relationship in freedom. The shame that shrouded his life compromised every experience of pleasure, rendering even curiosity and laughter suspect. Pleasures from every sense threatened to overwhelm—food, sight, sound (even music in church).

In chapter 10 of his *Confessions*, Augustine embarks on a long and torturous self-examination of the shameful actions that beset him. Eating and drinking are a constant struggle. He writes that "a dangerous pleasure accompanies" this necessary exercise in nourishment. He would like to be able to take food and drink "as medicine, without experiencing the accompanying pleasure." He likewise describes as "concupiscence of the eyes" the delight he takes in the sights and colors that absorb his attention, distracting him from God. He is wary of "glowing and beautiful colors. These things must not take hold on my soul; that is for God to do …" (10.34). He acknowledges the delight and pleasure that come in his love of God, but these are of a different kind. "What do I love when I love you?" He answers, "I do love a kind of light, melody, fragrance, food, touch when I love my God …" (10.6). With God these are delights that do not cease.

Curiosity is another concern. Early in *Confessions*, Augustine reflects on his desire to have his "ears tickled with false stories so they would itch all the more with curiosity" (1:10). Near the end of his memoir, Augustine includes curiosity in the list of the distractions that still beset him. Lust— the disordered seeking of every kind of pleasure—has ruined curiosity for him as well, rendering it "vain" and "morbid" (10:35). Augustine could not appreciate his own endless fascination with certain questions—the nature of the Trinity, the origin of a universal sinfulness—as instances of a dedicated and passionate curiosity.

Laughter presents a touching example of Augustine's difficulty with pleasure. He seemed unable to appreciate the ways that laughter refreshes and even heals the heart. For Augustine, laughter most often signaled ridicule or derision; he chronically feared being laughed at. On one occasion he expressed his concern that even God will laugh at him for his constant questioning. At his mother's death, Augustine weeps, even while fearful that others will "laugh him to scorn" for this expression of grief (9.12). For Augustine both laughter and tears were held hostage by shame, unable to serve as mediums of refreshing shared delight.

Desire, Passion, Pleasure

For Gregory, the dynamic image of God indwelling every human heart triggers a desire within each of us to find a way back to the source of this image. Desire, for Gregory, is, in the first instance, a healthy, God-created force within humans; it has not been rendered suspect as it has for

Augustine. (Desire in Gregory's Greek was the neutral term *epithumia;* in Augustine's Latin, it was translated as *concupiscentia,* which in English is most often rendered as *lust.*) For Gregory, the desire we experience in everyday life echoes the Creator's desire for our very existence. This constant human activity became the focus of Gregory's program for the education of desire.

Writing in Greek, Gregory spoke glowingly of *eros,* the dynamism that is desire seeking its eternal Source. As desire, *eros* has been described as "the homing instinct for God." For theologian Sarah Coakley, "Eros is agape *stretched out in longing* toward the divine goal." In one dazzling passage, Gregory brings together his understanding of love and desire: "Because Wisdom is speaking, love [*agape*] with all your heart and with all your strength, as much as you can. Desire as much as possible. And to these words I boldly add, fall in love [*eros*]!"

Gregory was convinced of "the moral character of the emotions" (J. Warren Smith) and argued that "the emotions can themselves be redeemed and even play an essential role in our salvation." Emotions, even painful and disruptive feelings, seemed to be part of what Gregory called "a divine pedagogy." For Gregory, "fear engenders obedience, anger courage, cowardice caution; the desiring faculty fosters in us the divine and pure pleasures."

Gregory argues that scripture shows that "the emotions can themselves be redeemed and even play an essential role in our salvation." For Gregory, this optimism also included the conviction that every beautiful thing in the world, by attracting our attention, draws us to the source of all beauty. "Hope always draws the soul from the beauty which is seen to what is beyond, always kindles the desire for the hidden through what is constantly perceived."

Augustine displays a very different perspective on desire and beauty. For him original sin had distorted human desire, reshaping it as lust and making it not only an unreliable resource in a Christian life but a spiritual threat to be avoided. Beautiful sights and sounds and tastes are more likely to distract us, even seduce us, than to lead us to God. This cautious view brought Augustine to a significant conclusion: "God alone may be enjoyed; creatures may not constitute the final resting place of our hearts and wills, but may only be used as instruments and not as ends in themselves." *Enjoyment* has a special meaning for Augustine:

"To enjoy is to cleave to something for its own sake ..." Augustine here defines enjoyment as a clinging attachment that is fitting only when it binds us to God. To *enjoy* anything else becomes a clinging that is akin to idolatry. Augustine defines the human person as "a rational soul *using* a mortal, earthly body." The body is little more than an instrument—and a dangerous one—to be *used* but not enjoyed in the soul's quest for God.

For Gregory, enjoyment and desire interact positively. Enjoyment of human beauty and earthly delights enkindles in us the desire to reach the Source of these blessings. Enjoyment and delight are instruments in the divine pedagogy by which we are drawn toward the Creator who is the beginning and end of all beauty.

One of the tragedies in Augustine's life—a tragedy passed down as an inheritance to generations of Christians in the West—was his inability to appreciate worldly beauty and sensual pleasure as experiences that may lead to a deeper relationship with God.

In *The City of God* (14:15) Augustine links pleasure with the lustful craving that he believes has perverted all human delights. "Pleasure is preceded by a certain appetite which is felt in the flesh like a craving, as hunger and thirst and that generative appetite which is commonly identified with the name lust ..." For Augustine, pleasure has fallen prey to lust; no innocent pleasures survive. This will also mean that for Augustine—and for those wounded by the legacy he has bequeathed—pleasure will be forever tainted by shame; to feel pleasure, wherever and however, will elicit a sense of shame and guilt. Moral theologian John Mahoney comments on the effects of this pessimism on Western Christianity: "Augustine of Hippo ... has perpetuated for centuries a mood of pessimism which moral theology is only beginning to shake off in this latter half of the twentieth century."

Restless for Eternal Beauty

A central theme of *The Confessions* is restlessness. The book begins with Augustine's confession of a holy disquiet: "[O]ur hearts are restless until they rest in you" (1:1). Augustine then turns to the unholy restlessness that marked his youthful years when an addictive desire for sex, honors, and even food drove him to a chronic restlessness. The memoir concludes with a prayer to God, who is "forever at rest" (13:38). The pivot of the

EVELYN EATON WHITEHEAD AND JAMES D. WHITEHEAD

entire story—his conversion to the Christian faith—takes place in a shift from extreme agitation just before this life-changing event to complete calm after his conversion. The narrative of Augustine's life traces his effort to resign the restlessness of his compulsive search for gratification and reshape this discomfort as a relentless desire for God.

For Augustine, genuine rest will be possible only at the end of life, just as the Creator's rest came only on the seventh day of Creation. In *The City of God*, written near the end of his life, Augustine returns again and again to the image of the Christian as a pilgrim—an exile, sojourner, and alien—in the worldly City of Man. Wounded by his own constitutional restlessness, Augustine was apparently unable to enjoy the refreshing rest that marks many lives: the deep satisfaction that comes at the end of a worthy project; the gratifying rest with one's partner after making love; the contentment that comes as companion of fatigue. These grace-filled delights were not to be part of his spirituality.

For Augustine, life is necessarily a pilgrimage through a land of broken promises and mirages of earthly delights. Restlessness kept Augustine's gaze on heaven, but it diminished his appreciation for creation. There can be great merit in being restless—not settling for less than the heart truly desires; there can be tragedy here as well—in remaining endlessly on edge, unable to commit or compromise, always looking past partial beauties and flawed humans toward an otherworldly ideal. This ideal can leave Christians uninterested in a world that, they have been cautioned, is passing away. And lacking interest, Christians may be unwilling to commit themselves to the healing of this broken world.

The Shape of Christian Conversion

Gregory and Augustine describe radically different paths of Christian conversion. For Gregory, conversion entails a gradual transformation as one progresses over a lifetime toward the Creator. He foresaw a slow and steady ascent toward God, guided by what he identified as a divine pedagogy. Like others in the Eastern Church, Gregory believed that all humans are being gathered up into their Creator—a process identified as divinization or deification. The biblical "Song of Songs," with its fusion of erotic desire and the love of God, serves as guide in the final stage of sanctification. Eros, for Gregory, names the desire that moves one constantly toward an eternal goal; this striving, for Gregory, is relentless but not restless.

Augustine's vision of conversion is profoundly different. Drawing on his own experience, he sees a wholehearted conversion to God as demanding a radical break with one's past. The turn to a fully committed love of God alone requires a rejection of one's former ways; nothing in this life is to be enjoyed but only to be used. An antagonism is a central dynamic in this picture: the sacred rejecting the secular; the City of God standing superior to and distant from the City of Man. This kind of dramatic conversion described, as well, the profound shift in the life of St. Paul, as well as that of Martin Luther. In Christian history, this more wrenching life change took on a heroic aspect. The more ordinary, everyday transformations of a Christian life—a path described and lived by Gregory—received less attention.

Who Will Be Saved?

Gregory believed that all humans, imbued as they are with an indelible image of their God, will ultimately and mysteriously be brought into a final eternal union with their loving Creator. Gregory describes "the final restoration which is expected to take place later in the kingdom of heaven of those who have suffered condemnation in Gehenna." In the final paragraph of his commentary on the "Song of Songs," written in the last years of his life, Gregory expands on this striking optimism: "Everyone is drawn to desire what they bless and praise ... All will look to the same goal, and every evil will be destroyed. God will be all in all, and all persons will be united together in fellowship of the Good, Christ Jesus our Lord, to whom be glory and power forever and ever. Amen."

For Augustine, the force of original sin marks all as guilty and every living person—even a newborn infant—as deserving of eternal punishment. In the Western Church, influenced by this perspective, infant baptism became an anxious requirement. The Eastern Church, embracing Gregory's significantly different understanding of ancestral sin, did not participate in this anxiety-driven concern.

Convinced by his own experience that no amount of human effort could contribute to a virtuous life, Augustine believed that God's grace—and only God's grace—could bring a soul to eternal salvation. And since this is the work solely of God's grace, we cannot know who among us has been predestined for salvation. But in Augustine's view, the vast mass of humankind would be consigned to eternal damnation. This dour view of predestination would engender centuries of rancorous and futile debate over "who will be saved."

J. Warren Smith, in his study of Gregory's thought, sums up the profound difference that separates Gregory and Augustine:

> Gregory of Nyssa's vision of the Christian life stands out, especially in contrast with Augustine's, for its realized eschatology. He has a confidence in the Christian's ability to achieve in this life a holiness that resembles the purity of heart and intimacy with communion with God that is the Christian's eschatological hope.

Conclusion

At the time of Augustine's death, the Roman Empire was in collapse as a long period of decline set in. Over the next six hundred years, his was the definitive theological voice to be heard. When creative reflection began again in Europe around AD 1000, Augustine's ideas assumed enormous authority. Augustine's theological legacy is mixed. The Christian community continues to benefit from his brilliant discussion of the Trinity and his appreciation of humanity's desperate thirst for God. Yet many Christians have inherited Augustine's convictions concerning the shamefulness of sexuality and its inherent linkage with sin, as his biased vision of sin and grace became the orthodox understanding in Western Christianity.

Theologians today muse on the influence of Augustine. For Margaret Miles, "The last four books of the Confessions (10–13) are, to me, profoundly sad." The erotic immediacy of the earlier chapters is set aside and replaced by authoritative and confident judgments. Miles believes that at that point Augustine had come to the place where "he insists now on loving only what he can love without fear of loss." Historian Peter Brown concludes his analysis of Augustine's life with the lament, "Seldom in the history of ideas has a man as great as Augustine or as very human, ended his life so much at the mercy of his own blind-spots."

John Mahoney, in his analysis of Augustine's moral theology and its influence in Western Christianity, observes, "It is saddening to note how the works of the great and loving man, with their passages of sublime beauty and moving eloquence, are often flawed by this note of melancholy, of disgust, and even of brutality, towards man in his sinfulness and weakness resulting from his initial fall from God's grace."

Today we are blessed with other visions of grace and sin, of the role of the senses and the emotions, of beauty and ordinary pleasures in the spiritual life. Gregory's wise and optimistic vision returns to us as "the future of our religious past."

Additional Resources

Charles Taylor discusses "the future of the religious past ... which is now available for us to retrieve" in his *A Secular Age*.

James O'Donnell has written an excellent critical biography of Augustine; see his *Augustine: A New Biography*. John Mahoney comments on Augustine's crucial distinction of enjoy/use in his *The Making of Moral Theology*.

Also see Martha Nussbaum, *Upheavals of Thought: The Intelligence of the Emotions*; Margaret Miles, *Desire and Delight: A New Reading of Augustine's Confessions*; and Peter Brown, *Augustine of Hippo: A Biography*.

For studies of Gregory, see J. Warren Smith's *Passion and Paradise: Human and Divine Emotion in the Thought of Gregory of Nyssa*. Also see Melvin Laird, "Under Solomon's Tutelage: The Education of Desire in the Homilies on the Song of Songs," in *Re-thinking Gregory of Nyssa*, and Sarah Coakley, "Pleasure Principles—Toward a Contemporary Theology of Desire," in *Harvard Divinity Bulletin*.

For Gregory of Nyssa's own writing, see *The Life of Moses* and *Commentary on the Song of Songs*.

PART THREE
Sexual Diversity

Chapter Eleven

Compassion, Justice, and Sexual Diversity

> *While he was still far off, his father saw him and was filled*
> *with compassion; he ran and put his arms around him and*
> *kissed him.* —Luke 15: 20

Jesus tells the story of a wayward son returning to the father he has sorely wronged. The homecoming takes a surprising turn. His father does not respond in anger or hold back until he has received an apology. He seems uninterested in pointing out the error of his son's ways to ensure the boy has learned his lesson. Instead he rushes out to meet his son, rejoicing in his return. Sensing the boy's humiliation and despair, the father's only concern is to welcome him home. He treats him as an honored guest and plans a great celebration.

This is what God is like, Jesus tells us. God acts toward us not as judge but as *abba*, an extravagantly loving parent. Our care for one another must show the same abundant concern. What God asks of us is not sacrifice but mercy. The lives of the godly will be marked not by the conspicuous good deeds of the righteous but by the humble compassion of those who respond to the needs of the world.

A Passionate Attachment

Compassion is an experience of intimacy. Ordinarily we think of compassion as commiseration: feeling the suffering of another person. But compassion has a more expansive meaning. With this emotion we enter into all the passions of one another—both delight and sorrow, joy and anger. By the bridge of imagination we cross over into another world of feeling. Like empathy, compassion gives us an uncanny capacity to participate in another person's inner world. We experience with other persons the excitement of their successes; we taste the sorrow that fills another's life. This extraordinary strength, which makes mutuality possible, enables us to enter another's life without intruding on his or her privacy or manipulating the person's emotions for our own purposes.

The arousal of compassion includes all the ways that our heart goes out to others. Nature, too, can call forth our compassionate response. Sitting silently on a shore we are drawn slowly into the mood of the breaking waves. Gradually our worry is replaced by other emotions. This compelling awareness of our union with nature and its unhurried rhythms is part of compassion.

Standing by a polluted stream we feel another emotion, one closer to the ordinary meaning of compassion. Contemplating this damaged resource, we experience regret and sorrow, tinged with a sense of responsibility. Polluting this stream soils our own life. Even if we do not live near the stream, we share its life and its ruin. This mood of regret stirs us to act, to do something to reverse this destruction.

Compassion has special poignancy when we are drawn to others in their injury and sorrow. The Latin word *misericordia* describes our compassion—we have a heart for those in misery. But compassion has another dynamic that invites our special attention. Identifying us with another's loss or pain, compassion makes us vulnerable, puts us at risk. When we are moved by people who are ill or in distress, we expose ourselves to their plight; we are disturbed. If we could avoid noticing other people's troubles, our life would be easier. But compassion opens us to the pain of the world, undermining our fragile sense of security.

This passion challenges the boundaries and barriers that make for a tidy social existence. Ensconced within the firm borders of our social standing or ethnic identity, we need not worry about the problems of others. Race, class, culture separate "us" from "them" and urge us to mind our own business and stay out of other people's affairs. But compassion transgresses these boundaries. We feel the anguish of the battered wife, and we sense the distress of those in prison. Suddenly, the hunger of the famine-stricken, the disorientation of the mentally ill, the frustration of the political outcast become experiences that are not alien. This is dangerous business. Such an arousal may lead us to question the barriers that separate us. Thus compassion often stands at the beginning of justice. Compassion leads us to recognize a relationship even with those who are not, on first glance, "like us." This emotion reminds us of a kinship that we can easily miss.

A well-known story in the Hebrew scriptures exposes the risky dynamic of compassion. The account of King Solomon's decision (1 Kings 3:16–28) is less about the king's wisdom than about a woman's compassion. Two pregnant women share the same household. Shortly after each delivers a child, one mother rolls over in her sleep, smothering her own baby. Awaking to find her child dead, she exchanges the infants, so that she now holds the surviving child as her own. But she does not fool the true mother, and a fight ensues over the child who is alive. Finally the women plead their case before the sage king. He brings an abrupt and startling verdict: let the child be divided, with each woman having half!

At this the woman who is the mother of the living child addresses the king, for she burns with compassion for her son. "If it please you, my lord," she says, "let them give her the child; only do not let them think of killing it!" The wise king can now give his real judgment: "Give the child to the first woman," he says, "and do not kill him. She is his mother."

This vivid story describes the inner workings of compassion. A woman is "stirred in her bowels"—the Hebrew word for compassion means, literally, a wrenching feeling in the gut. This visceral arousal responds to a "hidden kinship"—the woman recognizes her own child, though she cannot prove that the infant is hers. Solomon does not know the child's mother until the woman's compassion reveals the truth.

In her compassion the woman is put at risk. She faces not only her vulnerability before a powerful judge but the possible loss of her child. In the midst of this risky situation we see her compassion prompting her to act; she begs the king to give the child away! Her arousal brings forth fruit: her child is both spared and returned to her. And it is this woman's compassion that makes the king's wise decision possible.

Compassion is a social instinct that links us to others in feeling and action. This powerful emotion fails when we allow it to become simply a *private sentiment*. By isolating the arousal from effective action we privatize it. Then compassion degenerates into sentimentality. Our emotions are stirred but lead us nowhere. Our tears do not overflow into action; our feelings do not impel us to change anything. They remain stranded in the privacy of our heart. After a good cry, perhaps, we get on with our life. Then the rich virtue of compassion flounders in sentiment.

A second way that compassion fails is in pity, which often has about it the taint of condescension. Here our heart goes out in concern for others, but in going out we reach down. From a position of moral superiority we "descend" to feel sorry for the less fortunate. Reaching down with pity toward these lowly folk, we emphasize and reinforce the differences between us. In Fritz Perl's words, we care for those who are not "our own serious rivals."

Pity does not heal the gap between people but accentuates it. Our charity and our apparent care remind us of our advantage and defend our superiority. We take pity and show mercy to others in a context that includes no risk. The essential element of compassion—vulnerability—is curiously absent. We help others without identifying with them. Such pity is, at best, compassion compromised.

Learning to Be Kind

At first glance, compassion seems most closely linked with intimacy. But this strength also has much to do with justice. Compassionate actions join us in solidarity with those in difficult circumstances. These actions help us see through the barriers that separate and isolate us from one another. In crossing these boundaries, compassion opens us to a previously hidden kinship. Compassion reveals the *other* as our *neighbor*. Compassion teaches us to be kind.

We can, of course, be kind only to our own kind. We are not kin to aliens or strangers. Many of us have learned to see most other people as foreigners and outsiders. For compassion to be ignited in our hearts, we must find a new way of seeing. Often we first have to act "as if" those who are different—the first woman colleague at our work site, a resettled ethnic family just moved into our neighborhood, a member of the parish who is developmentally disabled—are, in truth, our kind. When we repeatedly act this way, we perform a kind of magic: these people begin to appear as "one of us"; their passions seem very similar to our own. We come to recognize a previously disguised kinship. Such an insight is an exercise in compassion; often this is the fountainhead of justice.

The connections between compassion and kinship become clear in the parable of the Good Samaritan (Luke 10:30–37). A man of Israel lies wounded on the roadside, a victim of highway robbery. Two of his own kind—a priest and a Levite—come upon the stricken man but pass him by. They recognize no kinship with him. He is an inconvenience, a tragic case, perhaps, but none of their affair. A third traveler approaches. He belongs to a tribe despised by the Jews; he is a Samaritan, an outsider, an enemy. This foreigner responds with compassion. Moved by the wounded man's plight, the stranger interrupts his journey. He dresses the man's wounds, takes him to an inn, and pays for his care. Ethnic hatred, national rivalry, a heritage of mutual suspicion are set aside in the face of this person's need.

Jesus offered this parable in answer to the question "Who is my neighbor?" The question raises a deeper concern: "Who has a right to my resources and a claim on my care?" Jesus responds by showing us how a neighbor acts and inviting us to do likewise.

The story Jesus tells is filled with paradox: Where we expect to see group solidarity in action, we find only indifference. Where hostility would not surprise us, we find genuine concern. In the actions of this outsider we see what constitutes kinship. Only he "was moved with compassion when he saw him." Our neighbor, then, is the person in need. "Our kind" are not just those linked to us by ties of blood or belief. Our kind are all those whose pain and hope we dare open ourselves to share. Compassion creates kinship. To answer the question "Who is my neighbor?" this parable responds, You can become a neighbor by letting yourself be moved to action by another's plight.

More than a surge of sympathy, compassion generates actions that heal. The generosity that stirs us to act toward others as our own kind can set off uncomfortable reflections. Compassion may not stop at the level of individual affection and charity. Recognizing another's plight, we may come to question how this suffering happened. Like empathy, compassion can become a revolutionary emotion. Its arousal can lead us to question social structures and cultural habits that institutionalize suffering and disguise human solidarity.

Jesus's life was emphatically about compassion. He made friends of many who seemed aliens: the foreign woman at the well, the tax collector hated by his peers, women of questionable reputation. As he embraced these unlikely persons as his own kind, Jesus continued that special vision of the world that was Israel's heritage. This legacy teaches us that the orphan and the widow are not outcasts but family; that foreigners and enemies are, finally, part of our community. Jesus called this fragile but persistent vision the kingdom of God. The Christian virtue of compassion impels us to reshape our world according to this vision.

Compassion and Sexuality

We might think that compassion and sexuality would be friends, since both are passionate responses linking us with other people. But, in fact, a fear of sexuality often limits our compassion. Every community—religious and ethnic—develops rules about sexual conduct. The group we belong to instructs us on the importance of marrying our own kind. We are taught the styles of sexual sharing that are acceptable among us. We learn that those who are sexually "different" must be avoided, even feared.

Andrew Solomon recalls his experience growing up gay in the 1960s, when homosexuality was seen as a crime, an illness, and a sin. He remembers an article in *Time* magazine in 1965: "Even in purely nonreligious terms, homosexuality represents a misuse of the sexual faculty. It is a pathetic little second-rate substitute for reality, a pitiable flight from life." The article continued, "[A]s such it deserves fairness, compassion, understanding and, when possible, treatment. But it deserves no encouragement, no glamorization, no rationalization, no fake status as minority martyrdom, no sophistry about simple differences in taste—and above all, no pretense that it is anything but a pernicious sickness."

This prejudicial attitude is being overcome. In the Christian community today we find recognitions of the kinship among homosexual, heterosexual, and transgender persons. Traditionally, religious discussions of sexual diversity often degenerated into conversations about "them," alien folk whose lives were consumed (it was said) in perverse and promiscuous behavior. These shadowy "others" were most emphatically excluded from our kind. Defensiveness distracted us from a simple truth, profound in its implications: we are the body of Christ, and some members of our body are transgender, lesbian, and gay.

Who are these members of the body of Christ? They are not *them*; they are us. They are our siblings and our children, our friends and our fellow parishioners. They are persons like us, striving to live generous lives of maturing faith. They are the ministers among us—priests, religious people, lay persons—who struggle to serve with integrity in a church that interprets the movement of their hearts as disordered and shameful.

When we listen well to the lives of these members of the community, we learn what should not come as surprising news: the transgender person seeks to be known "for who I really am," as do the rest of us. The lesbian or gay person is stirred with the same kinds of arousals and attractions that move the heterosexual person. These stirrings, quickened by a smile or a gesture, are more than "near occasions of sin." Like the arousals that stimulate our own loving, they are often near occasions of grace.

Arousal is the wellspring of sexuality for all of us. And for all of us these inclinations are filled with both promise and peril. For all of us, these arousals are subject to every conceivable perversion, as the human history of selfishness and sexual violence attests. For all of us, questions remain of how we will express our affection and respond to erotic arousal. We each face the challenge of finding a lifestyle and forging fidelities that are both adult and Christian.

The underlying experience of arousal is familiar to us all. We share a common passion. But sexually diverse Catholics have been instructed again and again in official church documents that, for them, erotic arousal is wrong. Quite apart from decisions about fruitful expression and responsible abstinence (decisions that confront every adult), the inclinations of their heart are judged to be perverse. Their feelings, we are told, do not and cannot resonate with the delight of God's creation. Their emotions are not a part of that human surge of affection that rescues us from our solitary journeys. Some arousals, we are instructed, should have no place in the life of a Christian. The only responsible choice is sexual abstinence, as part of a deeper self-denial.

Andrew Sullivan, himself a gay Catholic, writes of his own efforts to practice a kind of enforced "chastity," keeping his relationships superficial in an effort to "prevent passion from breaking out." Looking back on his strenuous, if failed, efforts to conform to the church's official instruction to gay Catholics, he muses that what resulted was "a theological austerity [that] became the essential complement to an emotional emptiness." Instead of a Christian life rooted in personal dignity and generosity, his life became, in his words, "a lie covered over by a career." Sullivan goes on to describe his conversion and the gradual reclaiming of his dignity: he remembers the "exhilaration I felt as my sexuality began to be incorporated into my life … a sense of being suffused at last with the possibility of being fully myself before those I loved and before God."

Compassion invites us to appreciate the urgency of the trans person's desire to embrace—in body and in social roles—the gender identity that is true to the deepest sense of self. Through compassion, we come to know that for a lesbian to feel erotic delight in the presence of another woman is not unnatural. For her this delight is the most natural feeling imaginable. She may deny these feelings, and this denial may grow into a habit of self-hatred. Then she embarks on a life that is truly disordered and unfruitful. Compassion also helps us recognize that a gay man does not *choose* to set aside his "natural, normal attraction" for women so that he can experience another more perverse kind of sexual excitement. The attraction he feels is natural and normal for him.

But if our awareness of gender diversity comes only from media accounts of sexual addiction and promiscuity, we may well have difficulty with compassion. Thoughts of two men being erotically aroused or of two women being sexually engaged may disgust or confuse us. Images of gender-confirming surgery may simply frighten us. These experiences seem so foreign; we cannot imagine anyone experiencing them in a way that is healthy or holy. In these instances, preoccupation with our own distress clouds our vision and defeats compassion.

A change of heart is taking place in the community of faith, even if this transformation is not yet evident in most official statements. We see its fruit in a new compassion shared among heterosexual, homosexual, and transgender Christians. Moral theologian Christina Traina observes, "In particular, there is much to learn about appropriate and holy uses of sensuality and non-coital sexuality from sources beyond theology of marriage: the psychology of touch, non-Christian cultures, and gay and lesbian Christians."

Community and Compassion

Where do we learn compassion? How does this virtue begin to grow in our life? At their best, Christian communities serve as nurturing sites. In prayer groups and ministry networks, in faith-sharing and other small group settings, people of faith experience community in practical and profound ways. As our lives intersect in these gatherings, we come to know each other more deeply. We can appreciate each other's enduring hopes and lingering wounds. Sharing these experiences of grace and failure, we participate in one another's passion. We touch lives so different from our own but, in their fragility and faith, so similar.

For many heterosexual Christians, compassion often takes root in sharing the faith journey of a transgender friend or a lesbian colleague or a gay family member. In this sharing we learn that their attractions and delights are very much like our own. The lesbian couple in our prayer group hopes to find fidelity and fruitfulness in love, as do the rest of us. The priest who is gay struggles to mature in his sexuality, just as the priest does who is heterosexual. Along with other mothers and fathers, the parents of transgender children yearn to find educational settings in which their children will thrive.

In the practical interplay of Christian community, we learn the shape of one another's hopes and passions. Through compassion we learn that we are more alike than different. To our Christian identity what matters most is not gender identity or sexual orientation or ethnic origin. What marks us as followers of Jesus is our behavior. From the first century onward Christians provoked the response, "See how they love one another!" The fruitfulness of this love is recognized in its respect, generosity, fidelity, and forgiveness.

Still, many churches struggle to have their stance toward sexual diversity shaped by such compassion. To some degree, this struggle reflects the hostility, discrimination, and outright violence toward homosexual and transgender persons that exist in our wider society. One expression of this hostility is *homophobia*—an irrational fear of homosexual behavior and homosexual persons, sometimes leading to hostile actions. Today *transphobia* is often used to identify the negative responses directed toward persons whose sense of self and public presentation challenge the gender dichotomy of male and female, masculine and feminine.

The term *phobia* is rooted in psychological discussions of fear. Some psychologists—as well as other advocates within the diversity community—are uncomfortable with the use of *homophobia* and *transphobia* to describe hostile attitudes and social behavior. As a psychological category, phobia designates a condition that may benefit from therapeutic intervention. But an individual burdened by a phobia is not seen to be personally responsible or "at fault." Take *claustrophobia*, for example: we may feel sorry for persons who are afraid of enclosed spaces, but we are not likely to blame them for their hesitance or hold them responsible for avoiding elevators. There is no legal or moral claim to be made. And as a psychological condition, a phobia is not easily eradicated. "I can't help it; this is just the way I feel." If homophobia and transphobia are understood simply as uncomfortable personal reactions, these social dynamics may not be recognized as deserving of public condemnation or legal restriction.

For this reason, many social advocates today suggest *heterosexism* as a more accurate description of prejudicial attitudes and hostile behaviors aroused by sexual diversity. Heterosexism—like racism, sexism, ageism—identifies a cultural bias that justifies discrimination against members of an identifiable social group. Heterosexism sees those who are sexually different or gender nonconforming as dangerous to society. Their aberrant behavior—even their self-identification—is morally wrong and must be stopped. Traditional gender roles are at risk: the acknowledgment of sexual diversity in our culture will lead to masculinized women and effeminate men. The stated concern is that the nuclear family—bedrock of society—will be destroyed.

Why do these prejudicial attitudes—and social dynamics—continue, even in the face of contradictory evidence that comes from the mature gay and lesbian and trans persons in our society, and often in our own families? Psychologists point to several functions that are served by social prejudice. There is an *existential* function: homophobia and heterosexism give people a way to shield themselves from disconcerting experiences of *otherness* and *differentness*. "These people are not like me!" If I can identify their "otherness" as unnatural and negative, I am freed from any responsibility to expand my understanding or perhaps even to change my mind.

Prejudice also serves a defensive function. Identifying sexual and gender diversity "out there" as deviant and dangerous protects me from looking more deeply at the ambiguity in my own experience. Perhaps my negative response to the public menace of sexual diversity will confirm (at least to me?) my solid heterosexual identity.

Expressions of bias and prejudice can also have a symbolic function.

Embracing the values and attitudes espoused by a group that is important to me reinforces my sense of belonging. Even if my own experience does not justify the prejudice, inclusion in the group may be sufficient reason to accept or at least go along with its biased perspective. In settings like this, members may judge that loyalty to the religious community requires that they adopt this negative appraisal of sexual diversity. Moral theologian Stephen Pope warns of this prejudicial effect: "The magisterium's message about gay sexual orientation is powerfully stigmatizing and dehumanizing. It is also at least tacitly, if not explicitly, liable to be used to support exactly the kinds of unjust discrimination that the church has repeatedly condemned."

How is this cultural bias of heterosexism overcome? Positive role models are particularly important. When those in influential social positions—political figures, religious leaders, respected media personalities—identify themselves as gay or lesbian or transgender, the witness of their lives challenges many of society's learned prejudices. Even more significant is being blessed with the witness of transgender and homosexual persons within one's family or circle of friends.

Another powerful antidote to the cultural bias of heterosexism comes in facing personal fears around sexuality. Being able to identify the hesitancies and perhaps even shame I carry in my own life is itself liberating. And often this growth in self-knowledge and self-acceptance frees me to learn from others, even from those whose self-identification and sexual behavior differ from mine. Becoming more comfortable with my own sexual experience, I am able to examine new evidence and understandings. I may not be persuaded by the arguments that challenge my personal values and moral convictions regarding sexuality and gender, but I am less susceptible to claims that are based on cultural prejudice and support social discrimination.

Legal recognition of same-gender marriages, nondiscrimination policies in adoptions, legal protections in regard to housing and employment—public opinion has been mixed in regard to these human rights advances. Public statements made by representatives of religious traditions and other respected organizations have had significant influence in these public debates. These denominations and organizations are not all in agreement regarding these public policies, but diverse public statements often force individuals to examine their own hesitancies. By reinforcing standards of justice and mercy in civic life, religious institutions can challenge negative cultural values and promote policies of dialogue and inclusion—even if they judge they must maintain institutional orthodoxy in their public statements.

To open the conversation with gay and lesbian and transgender members of our faith communities is perilous business. Such a compassionate conversation is only beginning to take place between church officials and sexually diverse Catholics. "The magisterium has yet to show any interest in engaging in dialogue with gay people or in listening to what they have to say about what it means to be gay and Catholic at the present time," Steven Pope laments. "Ironically, the magisterium has engaged in extensive official dialogue with Protestants, Jews, and Muslims, but it has yet to do so with gay Catholics." In such a conversation, long-held convictions may come under question. We may be forced to recognize that some of our attitudes and practices are shaped more by social bias than by the following of Christ. Deeper insight may arise into the demands of the Gospel, challenging the lifestyles of heterosexual, homosexual, and transgender persons alike. These conversations, even when undertaken with respect, promise to be disconcerting and disturbing to us all. But in a community that holds itself always open to God's Spirit, this conversation in faith must be undertaken.

In this effort to understand more deeply the links between sexuality and human dignity, we can be guided by Jesus, who asked his own friends the hard question "Who is my family?" He insisted that the powerful sway of bloodlines and ethnic purity cannot define belonging for those who live by faith. The boundaries of race and gender and sexual orientation, constructed and defended by every culture, come under question—as we learn to love our neighbor in the image of Jesus Christ.

Additional Resources

To access the theological analysis on this chapter's themes, see *Sexual Diversity and Catholicism: Toward a Development of Moral Theology*, edited by Patricia Jung and Joseph Coray; and Stephen Pope's essay "The Magisterium's Arguments against 'Same-Sex Marriage': An Ethical Analysis And Critique," in *Theological Studies*.

Also see James Keenan's discussion in "The Open Debate: Moral Theology and the Lives of Gay and Lesbian Persons," in *Theological Studies*.

Christina Traina's essay "Roman Catholic Resources for an Ethic of Sexuality" was prepared for the Common Ground Initiative in March 2004.

See the moving personal accounts of the experience of being gay in Andrew Sullivan, *Virtually Normal*; and Andrew Solomon, *Far From the Tree. Parents, Children, and the Search for Identity.*

Chapter Twelve

Transgender Lives: From Bewilderment to God's Extravagance

There is no longer Jew or Greek, there is no longer slave or free, there is no longer male or female; for all of you are one in Christ Jesus. —Galatians 3:28

For many of us, confronting questions of gender diversity is confusing.[1] Last month, a member of your parish whom you have known for years confided that he has begun hormone treatment. Charles described this decision as difficult but life-giving; he is now able to affirm this deepening conviction. At the core of his sense of self—his identity—Charles knows himself to be a woman. Asking for your support, Charles used the term *transgender*. You're not sure what that actually means, but it sounds ominous. The suggestion that you should now call her Clarissa left you speechless. How shall you respond to this information? How can you best support your friend through the transition ahead? What does the community of faith have to learn from—and to contribute to—this potentially perilous journey?

Gender Diversity: The Cultural Experience

Our understanding of gender—the images and expectations that define female and male—is always shaped by the surrounding culture. Western

---

1   For our working definitions of the vocabulary of gender diversity see the note at the end of this chapter.

cultures have long recognized that gender has a certain flexibility—even if only in fun. In Shakespeare's time, convention held that all characters in public dramas were played by men. So the character of Ophelia in Hamlet would be portrayed by a male actor in woman's clothes; this practice provided an initial cultural statement about gender roles and rules. And in a number of Shakespeare's plays—*Twelfth Night*, for example—we meet characters who switch genders for comedic effect. The gender-swaps in these scenarios are playful and without any challenge to larger cultural convention. Yet even in these make-believe plots, the malleability of gender is acknowledged. As we are entertained, we are invited to loosen our sense of the boundaries that divide the genders. On the stage this is all in fun. But play can be more than make-believe; it can test the leeway in our imagining of the world. However playful the presentation, subtle questions are being raised—can you imagine your life in the other gender?

Comedies from Shakespeare to Hollywood regularly turn to gender confusions as exercises in mistaken identity, with suggestions of sex adding spice to the scenario. In 1982 American moviegoers were treated to two variations on Shakespeare's playfulness. Julie Andrews, in the film *Victor/Victoria,* and Dustin Hoffman, in *Tootsie*, both portrayed gender-switching roles. With well-established celebrities at their core, these performances raised no serious questions of gender. These films were experiments in comedic cross-dressing rather than vehicles that raised substantive issues of gender identity.

A decade later the actress Tilda Swinton appeared in the film *Orlando.* In this adaptation of Virginia Woolf's allegorical novel, the central character lives for four hundred years, the first half as a man, the second half as a woman. Woolf's central theme is announced as, halfway through the film, Orlando's gender shifts from male to female. Swinton stands naked and speaks to the camera—"Same person; different sex." Her androgynous physique supports Swinton's role in embodying both genders. This film, then, raises the stakes higher, suggesting that such a transformation is conceivable. Its provocative mood seems to ask, "Want to make something of it?"

At the end of the last century, a yet more challenging movie appeared. In 2000 Hilary Swank won an Oscar as best actress in the film *Boys Don't Cry*. Here she is cast as a young woman determined to live as a man. Now we are not to be entertained by a comedy but instead confronted with a searing tragic story. For Swank's character in the film, the decision to present herself as a young man was met initially with violence and ultimately with her death. This film acknowledges that threats to the lives of transgender persons are not a laughing matter. The drama here raises disquieting questions of morality—less about the propriety of sexual conduct than about the violence so often provoked around questions of gender identity. As the United Methodist document *Made in God's Image* observes, "The problem is not in being different, but in living in a fearful, condemning world."

While Americans were going to the movies, real-life events also raised questions about gender diversity. In 1975, Richard Raskind underwent sex reassignment (now described as *gender-confirming*) surgery, becoming Renée Richards. As a male, Raskind excelled at tennis at the high school level and again at Yale University. Raskind had later served in the Navy and eventually became an eye surgeon. He married and fathered one son. After surgery, Renée Richards was denied entry as a woman in the 1976 US Tennis Open Tournament. She sued and, in a landmark judgment on transgender rights, the US Supreme Court ruled in her favor. More recently, Americans observed the publicity surrounding Chaz Bono, the transgender son of musical celebrities Sonny and Cher. Known earlier as Chastity Bono, he transitioned to living as a transman, completing gender-confirming surgery in 2008.

These developments, along with many similar experiences in both public and private lives, have led to an expanded cultural awareness. There is now a record of individuals who have successfully navigated a gender transition and of support groups to assist transgender persons in finding their way to a more integrated and healthy life. This information gives the members of the current generation a distinct advantage in approaching their own life decisions. Resources on the Internet connect those who had previously felt isolated and marginalized. The younger generation is also likely to suffer less from the religious condemnation that has haunted so many transgender persons in earlier generations. Our reflection here focuses on the continuing concerns of many trans individuals—across the generations—who await a more compassionate response from their culture and their religious traditions.

Most of us have grown up with a sense that gender divides naturally into "two and only two" categories: male and female. But if we pay attention, we notice that the human community displays a considerable variety—in both gender identity and self-presentation. Our society idolizes public figures who so thoroughly embody cultural gender ideals that they resemble caricatures of feminine and masculine: consider Dolly Parton and Arnold Schwarzenegger. Others in public life or the media live out more nuanced versions of humanity; here the musician Prince comes to mind. In our own communities, we are aware of effective male counselors and pastoral ministers whose demeanor—empathic, nurturing, comfortable with a range of emotions—does not fit the cultural stereotype of masculinity. And we meet women leaders whose determined style of decision-making and conflict-resolution distinguishes them from stereotypes of femininity. Such variety unsettles us only if we continue to embrace a rigid, nonnegotiable view of human nature.

Transgender Lives

> Gender identity ... is our own deeply held conviction and deeply felt inner awareness that we belong to one gender or the other. This awareness is firmly in place by the time we are five years old. Gender identity is private and internal. It is felt, not seen.   —Brown and Rounsley, True Selves

For the vast majority of individuals, inner gender identity and physical embodiment are well-matched. For transgender persons, that is not the case. "Transsexuals are individuals who strongly feel that they are, or ought to be, the opposite sex. The body they are born with does not match their own inner conviction and mental image of who they are or want to be. Nor are they comfortable with the gender role society expects them to play based on that body." The desire to harmonize physical appearance with their inner identity may find expression in cross-dressing—adopting clothing styles appropriate to their deeper sense of gender. For transsexuals, this decision "is not about playfulness, eroticism, fetishism, exhibitionism, or show business ... Transsexuals dress in the attire of the other gender solely as an outward expression of their core identity" (Brown and Rounsley).

Some individuals have, from early childhood, a strong sense of discomfort with the gender assigned to them at birth. Others may experience a sense of incongruity but are unable to define this until later in life. Whether in their twenties or fifties or even later, many transgender persons experience a deepening sense of disconnect between their assigned gender and their interior sense of themselves. Social pressure may have ensured that this realization was suppressed for decades. Often this disconnect is described as *gender dysphoria*: a person's "extreme discomfort with and sense of dissonance with the gender assigned at birth. The feeling is often persistent, continuing over a long period of time, and is not alleviated by other treatments, such as counseling" (Justin Tanis).

We are more aware today that gender and anatomy are not the same. And we are more conscious of the fact that gender is a blend of both social norms and inherent core identity. Every human fetus starts out with a similar set of gonads, thus with the potential to become either a girl or a boy. Later, under the influence of specific hormones, the fetus develops a vagina with a labia and clitoris, or a scrotum with a penis.

The first formation of gender, then, takes place before we are born, under the influence of prenatal hormones that influence the fetal brain. While we are afloat in our mother's womb, our tiny bodies and brains are awash in these hormones. Powerful chemicals prompt the gradual development of male or female genitalia, as well as inscribing a sense of gender identity in our infant brains. A developmental psychologist describes this evolution (Diane Ehrensaft, *Gender Born, Gender Made*):

> How do we get a boy brain or a girl brain? On the basis of our hormone receptors. It is determined by how we absorb the hormones that come to us as we float around in our mother's ... uterus ... Sometime in the first trimester, for example, the male fetus begins producing sex hormones that bathe his brain in testosterone for the rest of his gestation, producing a boy brain.

Most often the baby's anatomy will match the brain's sense of gender identity. But not always. Most transgender individuals as early as childhood experience a powerful and enduring dissonance between the gender that their body displays and their interior sense of themselves. For many, this search for gender integrity will entail a long and painful struggle. Spiritual health depends on their sorting out this disconnect and moving toward integrity in their experience of gender identity.

Hilary Howes describes her own struggle: "Blessed by our Creator with male genitalia and a female brain I struggled to relate to a society that saw me as male until age 40 when I transitioned to live as a woman. It was an authentic and mid-life transition to integrate my mind and body that many who knew me supported and even called courageous, inspiring and ethical." Howes acknowledges the support she received from many who were close to her. She goes on to report the judgmental attitude of many others: "But this uniquely personal act through the eyes of the 99.5 percent of people who are blessed to have their gender and sex match has been seen as a political act, a psychological disorder, a character flaw, a weakness, a perversion and a sin."

With or without support, many transgender persons begin the process of *transition,* moving toward a more public embrace of the gender that fits the inner sense of self. In the transgender community *transition* is understood as a verb—the courageous effort to integrate one's inner gender identity with outward gender expression. Psychologist Mildred Brown describes this movement in her clients: "Transitioning—going from living as one gender to living as the other—is incredibly exciting for transsexuals." Now the person "is free to live in the appropriate gender role and to move toward becoming whole." The good news is that stories of successful transition—from the gender assigned at birth to the gender that fits the person's abiding sense of identity—are becoming more common and more widely available. Hilary Howes describes the fruit of her transition: "Transitioning allows us to share with society the gender personality that we have been from the start. It avoids the false-selves we developed to live as others expected us to, based on our external bodies."

This transition may begin as early as childhood, with or without the support of family members and helping professionals. Some trans persons begin their transition in young adulthood, as they move toward greater independence in lifestyle and work. Perhaps more traumatic is the transition in midlife, for persons deeply embedded in public commitments of marriage and career. But growing evidence suggests that when no action is taken (due to either personal hesitancies or external threats), serious depression is likely to follow. Melissa described this movement in her own life. "My feelings about myself quickly progressed from frustration to anger, to self-hatred, to worthlessness, to my possibly being a sinner who was doomed to spend eternity in hell. My life wasn't worth living, and I couldn't stand myself any longer. Thoughts of suicide, which I also knew to be morally wrong, began to grow" (communication to authors).

In transition, a person takes steps to give more public expression to the inner sense of self. Usually the shift is not an abrupt movement from one social identity to another but a gradual—often tentative—effort to adopt the behavior patterns that better fit the authentic sense of self. And for some, this shift does not demand a rejection of one's former self. A trans person explains her desire to bring with her the best of her past that was lived as John: "I'm not trying to make John disappear … there's a lot of useful things in John. He gets the job done, and he got me this far, but that's not who I am now."

For some transgender persons, an important dimension of their transition is hormone treatment (estrogen or testosterone) that influences muscular shape, facial hair, and other secondary sex characteristics. Those who can afford it may also pursue the painful and expensive procedures of gender-confirming surgery. Hilary Howes observes, "Any United States transsexual who gets a surgical procedure does so after psychological evaluation, much soul searching … The vast majority of transsexuals never have surgery because the expense is only covered by a handful of healthcare policies."

Coming Out: Three Passages to the Light

Those who experience a powerful disconnect between their deepest sense of gender identity and the evidence that their physical anatomy presents to the world face a daunting challenge. How can they survive and thrive in a public world that enforces strict gender lines and threatens violence toward those who do not conform? Transgender persons experience competing impulses: *Should I, for my own safety, remain in hiding? Must I travel through life in disguise, pretending to be someone I am not? Is there some way for me to respond, in integrity and with whatever courage I can summon, to the deeper hope to be seen and even cherished for who I am?*

Resolving such a dilemma becomes for many trans persons a spiritual journey marked by significant passages. For some, this becomes also a journey of faith. The Bible introduces us to religious ancestors who escaped slavery in Egypt to find new life only by passing through a harrowing desert. In our own lives we can expect similar desert journeys: periods of loss, times of letting go, seasons of absence when we are bereft of our accustomed comfort and confidence. Disorientation and vulnerability are expectable companions on the journey of faith. "A land flowing with milk and honey" often lies beyond a stark and empty place.

For a transgender person, the journey toward a fuller life often begins "in the closet." The closet is an enclosure, a hiding place that confines even as it protects. In this shadowy space we may find a secure anonymity, but there will be little growth. A transgender man describes this confinement: "It seems like most of my adult life has been spent in a locked room or a closet, and even though the closet didn't feel secure, at least I felt like I owned it. I knew how the lock and key worked and how to keep people out and at a distance." A trans friend, speaking for many, has observed, "It is exhausting to exist and stay hidden." Exhausted by secrecy or shame, some people turn to the false comfort of alcohol and drugs to see them through the night. And in time, despair may drive the search for ways to end this dark night, once and for all. But for those who are fortunate, the confinement of the closet can be set aside. Its safety comes at too high a price. Now the voice of conscience insists it is time to grow, to risk a new and different life.

But potent social forces conspire to keep a person in the closet. Family and culture sometimes recommend a denial of reality, encouraging the transgender person to settle for a superficial life. Initial efforts at honest self-disclosure may be met with strong resistance. Church communities often conspire in this refusal to recognize the truth that lies within. If one is to belong, multiple disguises are demanded. Sometimes a transgender person may enter into a conventional marriage, hoping to overcome her "aberrant" desire. Another may choose a career that will emphasize a male identity: becoming a surgeon, or entering the military, or training as an engineer. Here again the hope is to silence or at least to mute an inner feminine voice. But a drive deep in human nature, more potent than shame or addiction, moves many transsexuals to search out an integration long desired—the harmony of inner self and outer self-expression. By the grace of God, a person begins the liberating journey to heal this debilitating dissonance.

A first interior passage : the movement toward self-acceptance. In this spiritual transition a trans individual enters a perilous passage, "coming out" in a conscious acceptance and embrace of *who I am.* Recognizing *this is how God has made me* brings confidence, even consolation. "Beloved of God, I am not a freak." For many, this initial passage has the psychological force of a conversion: from self-denial with its patterns of disguise and deception toward an appreciation and even celebration of who one is. This hard-won acceptance can shape a sense of vocation: I am called by God *as I am.* Personal integrity finds its foundation here.

Sometimes it is an external crisis that brings transgender persons to their knees in surrender to the truth of who they are. For Linda it was a nervous breakdown, and as she lay in the psychiatric unit of the hospital, she heard herself saying to God, "I give up! I can't fight this anymore. Please help me." For others, the inner fight simply wears them down and from within themselves they realize they must claim their truth, whatever the cost. Often this first passage is a matter of two steps forward and one step backward. For many transsexuals there comes a point when they can say, "This is who I am and who I will always be. I want to find a way to befriend this and stop fighting it" (communication to authors).

Mildred Brown comments, "Coming out to oneself can be a slow and difficult process, but most report that it is a positive and personally satisfying experience—one that provides a tremendous sense of freedom and renewed strength." This interior passage usually precedes decisions about public expression, though these decisions often follow from the interior affirmation of self-worth.

A second passage: widening the circle of intimacy. We are social creatures, who long to be known as we are—to have our identity affirmed by those closest to us. So the private passage of self-acceptance does not suffice for most persons. As self-confidence grows, a transgender person often becomes eager to share this enlivened identity with some of those with whom one is emotionally connected—a member of one's family, a longtime friend.

It is often in the protected sanctuary provided by a trusted friend or spiritual guide that a transgender person first feels free to acknowledge and test out new possibilities for a more integrated life. A counselor or spiritual director may also serve as a crucial companion as a person faces the challenge of coming out to family members. In these intimate settings, the transgender person is often confronted by inner and outer voices that insist, "You are just being selfish!" This accusation, devoid of empathy, assumes that a person is acting on a mere whim, a willful desire to transgress sacred laws of nature—and cause embarrassment to the family as well. A therapist or spiritual guide can assist the transgender person in conversation with the more accepting members of one's family, while reminding the individual that parents will need time to grieve the loss of a daughter as they accept their son. Hopefully, in time family members may come to realize that their transgender child or sibling remains the same person. Despite a perhaps shocking change in appearance and self-presentation, the person they have known all these years is still with them.

This second passage may include practical experiments in gender self-presentation. Many transgender persons now start to explore hormone treatments or cosmetic procedures to bring the body's shape into greater conformity with the underlying gender identity. A number of transgender persons attest to the thrill of finally seeing in the mirror their external appearance, which now matches their interior sense of gender.

A third passage moves into the wider public realm. After the initial passage of self-acceptance and the second passage of being known within one's intimate circle, some trans persons take steps to "come out" in the wider public arena of the workplace or faith community. A spiritual guide tells of sharing a meal in a restaurant with a counselee, now dressed in her newly appropriate gender wardrobe. In this semipublic experiment—both thrilling and terrifying—the transgender person is able to make "a test run" in exploring her new identity.

There are, of course, many reasons not to move toward this more public passage—seeking to avoid discrimination or violence rank high on this list. Yet for some transgender persons, the desire to be known *as I am* in wider areas of life is compelling. Here the role of a welcoming community becomes central. For one professional, well-known and respected in her work site, such a public coming out will be manageable. A skillful announcement of the transition (for instance, an early conversation with one's employer or a notice distributed among office colleagues) may help to prepare other people for the unavoidable shock of the transition. A ministry colleague recalls an ER physician who transitioned on the job. Her obvious skills and the professionalism of the ER staff helped make this a smooth transition. But for every story of successful change, there are many other tales of discrimination and rejection. And quite apart from the challenges of family and work site are the everyday encounters that must somehow be managed. The authors of *True Selves* recount how one transsexual simply showed up, after transitioning, at the garage to reclaim her just-repaired ten-year-old Porsche: whatever the mechanic thought about her, she had decided, it would be more distressing to try to find a new mechanic.

The Grace of Bewilderment

Becoming more aware of transgender persons in our families and communities, we may recognize a theme that we have met again and again in scripture: the harrowing movement from bewilderment to a celebration of God's extravagance. Bewilderment is defined as "confusion arising from losing one's way; mental confusion from inability to grasp or see one's way through a maze or tangle of impressions or ideas." The psychological experience of bewilderment includes awareness that "much of what we are or can aspire to be arises from circumstances beyond our control." Religious scholar Lee Yearley speaks of bewilderment as a virtue that "corrects the inclination to unwarranted certainty." Undermining our unwarranted certainty, bewilderment stands as a portal to humility. Distressing as this emotion is for individuals, institutions are even more disturbed. Religious leaders are loath to acknowledge bewilderment, lest this suggest personal weakness or corporate uncertainty. In the face of such stout defense of certitude, it is useful to recall the biblical support for this salutary mood.

The *Oxford English Dictionary* defines *bewilder* as "to lose in pathless places, to confound for want of a plain road." Such disorientation is a recurring theme in our religious tradition. Our earliest ancestors, escaping from slavery, found themselves in a wilderness.

> Then Moses ordered Israel to set out for the Red Sea, and they went into the wilderness of Shur. They went three days in the wilderness and found not water … The whole congregation of the Israelites complained against Moses and Aaron in the wilderness … "[Y]ou have brought us out into this wilderness to kill this whole assembly with hunger" (Exodus 15:22; 16:2, 3).

141

The theme of wilderness as an expectable sojourn on the spiritual journey reappears early in Mark's Gospel: "And the spirit immediately drove [Jesus] out into the wilderness. He was in the wilderness for forty days, tempted by Satan; and he was with the wild beasts; and the angels waited on him" (Mark 1:12). The biblical witness: The wilderness will not defeat you; do not turn back to the false comforts of slavery or to the blandishments of Satan. There will be life on the other side of this desert experience. Thus scripture reminds us that bewilderment is an expectable disturbance in the journey of faith.

Bewilderment is both a distressing and a valuable emotion. It names the feeling we experience when confronting the puzzling world that derails the confidence we have counted on. The self-righteous and the "saved" will likely see this emotion as moral weakness and lack of faith. Yet psychologists recognize this disorienting experience as a dynamic in our growth toward maturity; never to experience this feeling suggests we have lingered too close to home. Catholic philosopher Charles Taylor goes further, reflecting on a danger that may beset Catholics in the face of a rapidly changing world: "[T]he danger is that we will not be sufficiently bewildered …" His hope for Christians in a late-modern world is that "after initial (and let's face it, continuing) bewilderment, we would gradually find our voice from within the achievements of modernity" and bring the gifts of Christian faith to this changing world.

An Invitation to Humility

Bewilderment disarms us of long-cherished convictions and biases. In its sway, we become less self-assured. Here the virtue of humility arises, opening us again to mystery. "Humility is the ancient ever-new virtue that keeps us rooted in our earthiness and able to savor our human limits as gifts." Theologians remind us that our attempts to make sense of divine reality will be "always and inevitably imperfect, a peering through a dark glass of human limited intelligence and limited language, such that no one glimpse or expression can encompass or exhaust the divine reality …" As a people pledged to the mystery of God, humility should be our default attitude.

James Keenan cautions us about our impressive ignorance of the natural world: "Nature is a complex and unfolding system whose finality, development, and ways of interacting are grasped only partially—though not arbitrarily—by human insight." He concludes, "The totality of human nature in its whole richness, with its potential and capacities which are yet to be awakened, can be grasped only in history, not by an aprioristic affirmation about its essence."

Philosopher Susan Neiman comments on our impressive ignorance of the human realm as well: "We know, in general, quite a lot. We know that our capacities for error are great, and our capacities for self-deception even greater. We know that our motives are usually mixed ... We also know that we are free." She concludes, "Given all that we know, humility about what we don't know is ... a moral imperative."

Often *male* and *female* have been presented as "clear and distinct" realities, understood in an either/or dichotomy that was well-defended by cultural and religious decrees. Today we are aware that human nature is more variable—even more mysterious—than we had once assumed.

Ongoing research—physiological and psychological—confirms that gender is experienced and expressed along a wide spectrum. Psychotherapist Amy Bloom comments on the enduring bias that obstructs this more accurate and generous view. "The notion that gender has a continuum, a fluid range of possibilities, seems to produce such anxious rigidity in many of us that we ignore everything we've learned through our own lives about the complexities of men and women." As we gain a more accurate understanding of gender's continuum, transgender members of the human community may be recognized no longer as "mistakes" of biology or genetics but as evidence of this extravagant creation.

Discovering God's Extravagance

Surviving our bewilderment and embracing anew the virtue of humility, we open ourselves to a signature feature of creation—God's extravagance. We inhabit a universe that dazzles with its size and diversity. Astronomers inform us of the unthinkable enormity of multiple galaxies and innumerable black holes. The director of the Vatican observatory has noted that there are 10^{22} stars in the universe (this abbreviation means the number ten followed by twenty-two zeros). Such outsized numbers tax our comprehension. We learn that the universe—and our planet itself—existed for billions of years before human participation. And biologists tell us of the myriad forms of life that populate our own world even now; for example, two hundred species of ants have been identified. How to explain this abundance? The dazzling shapes and colors of tropical fish collected in an aquarium overwhelm our senses. Then there is the annual profusion of acorns that every autumn fall from a single oak tree. The lavishness of creation assaults our minds and challenges our comprehension. A boundless generosity is on exhibit throughout our world. What are we to make of this extravagance? How are we to honor its generosity?

The life experience of transgender persons also draws us into this story of God's extravagance. A friend or family member begins the transition—psychological, social, perhaps physical as well—toward deeper self-understanding. Now we are privileged to be part of this journey toward wholeness, one that leads beyond conventional categories of gender into another experience of personhood. It is here that we may meet the God of extravagance.

The Discernment of Spirits

The transgender person's journey from self-denial toward deeper authenticity finds support in the traditional Christian exercise of "discernment of spirits." In the Ignatian Spiritual Exercises, discernment is understood as "a specifically spiritual and Christian way of reading reality … It aims at more than a human sifting of the shadows and lights of a social environment. It seeks to recognize the presence of the Spirit within the human." Discernment requires paying close attention to the interior movements of our heart, especially when we are confused or in conflict. Thus the discernment process begins with an examination of painful emotions—the personal regret or guilt or shame that prompts our desire for new life. And this spiritual exercise proceeds with the confidence that if we listen well to the various voices or "spirits" moving through our hearts, we will be able to distinguish those that lead toward life and those that distract us from our true path.

Jolie, herself a trans woman, describes the challenges of this spiritual journey:

> Transsexual persons share an experience of hiding their
> identity and sometimes going to extreme lengths to

conform to the expectations of their families, schools, employers. When a transsexual person makes the intrinsically spiritual decision to openly embrace their true identity, they confront all of the obstacles that have threatened their lives and livelihood.

She continues: "This transition takes on enormous dimensions in their lives that change and rearrange all other priorities. Transsexual people become spiritual warriors and true-believer disciples like reformed smokers but magnified by a force of ten thousand. Often newly revealed transsexual people come across as 'bewilderingly' intense and single focused on this one goal, insisting on identities that other people have no clue how to recognize. Transition for the transsexual becomes the 'kingdom of God' as in the quote 'The Kingdom of God is like treasure a man finds in a field. The man goes out and sells everything he has to buy that one field.' Transition processes take on the urgency of having air to breathe."

Jolie concludes, "This process is a uniquely mystical and spiritual journey to find one's true soul in relationship with an entire universe. It is maddening, bruising and even dangerous for the transsexual person who chooses this path. It is a crucible of fire that some may survive and that quite literally far too many do not" (communication to authors).

Dawn describes the fruit of her own spiritual discernment:

> Coming to terms with my religious faith at last freed me to move forward with my transition. Instead of waking each morning regretting that God did not take me during the night, I am anxious to get up and face the day, for being alive is now a miracle instead of a curse. I like what I see in the mirror, a fifty-plus woman who will at last be able to enjoy her true spirit. My friends tell me they can see the difference in my face and hear the happiness in my voice.

She concludes, "I cannot change my faith and I cannot change my being transsexual. I can only choose to die trying to live a lie, or live the way that makes my soul sing" (communication to authors).

A sustained process of discernment leads to a peaceful decision and a mood of consolation. Justin Tanis, writing of his own gender transition, describes a movement from restless desolation toward peaceful self-acceptance: "[S]o many of my colleagues have commented to me that I am so much more peaceful and calm in the years since I transitioned. They say I always seemed angry, driven and unhappy before." He had had "a sense of spiritual restlessness because I had not found a home within myself where I could be genuinely myself."

For the whole community, discernment includes an examination of our language. We realize we are responsible for how we speak. How shall we speak of the lives of transgender persons? An earlier vocabulary in use often identified these members of the human community as "abnormal," as unnatural freaks or monsters. Today, with the benefit of better scientific information and deeper pastoral insight, we will build a vocabulary of diversity that is more inclusive and more compassionate—and more accurate.

In the Spiritual Exercises Ignatius Loyola counsels us: "Pray for what you desire." As Christians we dare to connect God's desires with our own best hopes. God's ambition for our lives lies half-hidden in the desires that already stir our hearts. In the inevitable ambiguities of our search, we can trust that God's desire for us does not conflict with the best interests of our deepest and truest selves. A leading authority on Ignatian spirituality comments: "God our Creator and Lord writes God's hopes into our desiring. If our hearts are made for God, then God has planted deep, deep desires for God in our hearts."

Conclusion

> "Nothing human is alien to me."
> (*Humani nihil a me alienum.*)
> —Terence, Roman playwright in the second century BCE

Hilary Howes observes, "[O]ur theology calls us to follow our consciences, accept mystery and love one another without exception. Reaching out to my marginalized extreme minority is not only possible but enriches our spiritual life." She concludes, "I hope that [Christians] would look at the body of scientific and medical evidence to develop a loving acceptance of those of us with this variation." Finally, she adds, "I understand that my journey, though personal, touches that which is universal about gender for everyone … looking at everything as us and them, black and white, male or female, is limiting and dangerous. Ultimately, welcoming the mystery of diversity in God's plan is the healing for our church for which I most hope."

Justin Tanis writes of "the sacredness of transformations." We are changelings, all—from embryonic fetuses to unruly adolescents to sober adults. We evolve and discover ever new potential lying half-hidden in our hearts. The ritual of baptism, with its symbolic rebirth and renaming, seeks to honor something of our changeling nature. St. Paul sought to express the radical transformations that accompany Christian faith. "There is no longer Jew or Greek, there is no longer slave or free; there is no longer male or female; for all of you are one in Christ Jesus" (Galatians 3:28).

Many of us struggle to believe Paul's prophetic declaration. In a life of discipleship as we follow the path of Jesus Christ, cultural differences and prejudices begin to fall away. We come to see that human nature is not simply a biologically determined essence. We become more capable of welcoming those who differ from us, even those whom society has rejected. In our support for transsexual Christians, compassion and justice embrace as we glimpse new intimations of the coming kingdom of God.

The spiritual journey often moves from bewilderment to recognition of God's extravagance. Sometimes this extravagance itself is more than we can fathom—is itself bewildering. But there is now a different feel to this emotion. A desert bewilders as we find no signs to guide our movement; we stumble in confusion and disorientation. But the bewilderment we experience when confronted with God's extravagance on display in the lives of our transgender sisters and brothers does not distress but bedazzles us. We do not search for a safe exit from our confusion but for a place to kneel.

A Note on the Language of Gender Diversity

In the current discussion of gender, definitions are regularly contested and revised. We offer here several "working definitions" that guide our own reflections.

Transgender: This term often serves as an umbrella concept that includes all persons who are gender-variant; that is, who do not conform to social expectations about masculine and feminine. This includes, among others, transsexuals, cross-dressers, and intersex persons. In this essay we follow the usage recommended by Diane Ehrensaft in *Gender Born, Gender Made*: "I am using *transgender* in its broadest definition, which is any [person] who strays from the traditional binary male-female gender model" (p. 58).

Gender dysphoria is defined as a person's "extreme discomfort with and sense of dissonance with the gender assigned at birth. The feeling is often persistent, continuing over a long period of time, and is not alleviated by other treatments, such as counseling." (See Justin Tanis, *Transgendered: Theology, Ministry and Communities of Faith*, p. 20.)

Transsexual: This word describes those transgender persons who experience a strong disconnect between the gender they were assigned at birth and their enduring inner sense of gender identity. These persons often experience a desire to transition to a self-presentation that harmonizes with this inner sense of identity. This may or may not include hormone treatment and gender-confirming surgery.

Cross-dressers: Persons who receive satisfaction and pleasure from dressing as the opposite gender. "The term generally is used for heterosexual men who dress as women, usually in their own homes, although also at events set up for this purpose" (Tanis, p. 22). This term also includes drag queens and others whose gender bending is more a question of theatrical performance rather than gender identity. An earlier term, *transvestite*, is today considered derogatory.

Intersex: This term describes persons who are born with ambiguous genitals; that is, with physical, hormonal, or chromosomal aspects of more than one sex. Such persons were traditionally referred to as hermaphrodites. *Middlesex,* a Pulitzer Prize–winning novel by Jeffrey Eugenides, offers a sensitive portrait of a young girl, born intersex, as she becomes aware at the onset of puberty of her genital ambiguity and, over the course of the story, succeeds in transitioning to the male gender.

Additional Resources

True Selves: Understanding Transsexualism, by Mildred Brown and Chloe Ann Rounsley, is regarded as one of the best resources on transgender lives. In *Gender Born, Gender Made*, Diane Ehrensaft focuses on effective care for transgender children and their families. Also see Stephanie Brill and Rachel Pepper, *The Transgender Child*, and Genny Beemyn and Susan Rankin, *The Lives of Transgender People*.

Justin Tanis's valuable discussion appears in *Transgendered: Theology, Ministry and Communities of Faith*. Hilary Howes's comment here is drawn from her essay "To Be or Not to Be: A Catholic Transsexual Speaks," in *Conscience*.

Lee Yearley's comment on the themes of bewilderment and humility is found in "Ethics of Bewilderment," *Journal of Religious Ethics*. See also Avis Clendenen, "A Rare Humility and a Future-Facing Myth," *Review for Religious*, and Charles Taylor, "A Catholic Modernity?" in his book *Dilemmas and Connections*.

Also see James Keenan, *A History of Catholic Moral Theology in the Twentieth Century*, and Susan Neiman's *Moral Clarity*.

An earlier version of this chapter appeared as "Transgender Lives: From Bewilderment to God's Extravagance," in *Pastoral Psychology*, April 2014, 63:171–184.

Chapter Thirteen

Born in Grace: Gender-Diverse Children

For it is you who formed my inward part; you knit me
together in my mother's womb. I praise you, for I am
fearfully and wonderfully made. Psalm 139:13

For centuries Christians, guided by St. Augustine, have believed that humans are born in sin. A child begins life marked by an original fault, inherited from our ancestors Adam and Eve. This depravity stains our souls and is also registered in our bodies—particularly in the lustful urges that often lead to the sins of the flesh. We begin life as damaged goods.

Many Christians today turn away from this dire interpretation of the human condition. They recall an earlier scriptural conviction—that we are born in grace. As the events of the biblical creation story evolve, we read of the Creator's repeated judgment: "This is good!" Here at the start of creation there is no sin. Sin would follow soon enough, but it did not share the stage at the beginning. The biblical account of our origins also records a dazzling diversity in the array of crawling, flying, swimming creatures. In its first exuberant stirrings, "This is good" applied to all of God's handiwork. This recognition of both creation's goodness and its profound diversity grounds our reflection on gender-diverse children.

Gender-Diverse Children

Being posed for a photograph in a red velvet dress, both
the photographer and my mother had difficulty getting

me to look up and smile, to hold the phone next to my ear as if I were talking on it. They wanted me to look up, but I kept looking down at the expanse of brightly colored dress, white leather baby shoes, and especially the itchy strangeness on my upper arms where the gathers held the fabric in bunches. I was aware of one thing: This was all wrong. The date on the photo puts my age at 22 months (David, communication to authors).

In many faith communities and nearly every school system, there are families facing questions of gender identity. As most parents know, children often go through a period of *gender experimentation*—wanting to dress like the parent of the opposite gender or insisting on a new name as part of a tomboy stage. But for some children this behavior is not just a passing phase or simply evidence of a child resisting parents' authority. Something more is involved. A three-year-old daughter insists, again and again, that she is really a boy. A four-year-old son plays with his older sister's clothes and wants to be called by a girls' name. What is happening here? Psychologists stress that "if a toddler goes through a phase of insisting they are the opposite gender of their birth sex, and if this 'phase' doesn't end, it's not a phase" (Brill and Pepper, *The Transgender Child*).

A continuing sense of disconnect throws the child off stride, provoking inner turmoil and self-doubt. The child longs to be able to "fit in" with the expectations of parents and others but cannot do so. These pressures leave children and adolescents with an abiding sense of alienation, from themselves and from the social settings (parental home and extended family, neighborhood, and school) where they are desperate to feel included. But these children often have no acceptable way to deal with their distress. In the abstract language of psychology, "they have difficulty integrating their emotions and cross-gender inclinations into the narrow parameters of our culture's rigid two-gender system."

In describing her early transgender experience, filmmaker Lana Wachowski recalls the confusions she experienced—as the young Larry— in responding to gender expectations at school. As students assembled before class, boys in one line and girls in another, Larry often found himself standing between the two rows: "I think some unconscious part

FRUITFUL EMBRACES

of me figured I was exactly where I belonged: betwixt." Needless to say, years of bullying followed for the boy who stood "betwixt."

Dawn describes similar turmoil in her childhood. "As a small boy I insisted on playing with girls at school recess. The parish priest was called to make things clear. 'You must play with the other boys. That is how you will learn to be the man God wants you to be.' When I continued to protest, the priest added, 'it is sinful to not do what God wants us to. God made you a boy and you must be a boy. You must put away these sinful thoughts and pray that God gives you the strength to obey his will for you. If you don't, you will go to hell.' Then he moved out from behind the desk and walked toward me, exposing the wooden paddle he often used to reinforce his commands. 'I'm going to help you remember this lesson, help you understand the pain of disobeying God's will.'" Looking back, Dawn recalls, "I began to pray the rosary each night asking Mary to help me feel happy that I was born a boy. But still in my heart, I really hoped I would wake up a girl. But all the prayer did not help. I failed at being the boy I [was] supposed to be" (communication to authors).

Strategies of Imagination

Childhood is a season of fantasy and make-believe. Many trans children turn to the interior resource of imagination to help them survive the dissonance they are experiencing. Some fantasize that when they grow up they will finally emerge in the opposite gender. Others fall asleep praying that they will awake in the morning as "the right sex"—in a body that fits their inner sense of self. Looking back forty years, David recalls a favorite fantasy: "When the bus pulled up to my elementary school in the first grade, the fantasy I indulged as I got off and plodded toward my classroom was that today might be the day when my mother would receive a phone call from the hospital where I was born. They would explain, very apologetically, that there had been a mistake; their daughter was, in fact, a boy." Finally, he dreamed, "people would no longer attempt to correct my behavior, my stance, or my mannerisms; these attributes might even be encouraged. I could wear clothes that suited me, play with toys that suited me, and I would finally be at ease" (communication to authors).

The authors of the valuable resource book *True Selves* recount the story of the six-year-old child who is reminded to make a wish as she

153

blows out the candles on a birthday cake. Excited by this possibility, the child blurts out, "I wish I will grow a penis by my next birthday." Another child discovered that in make-believe games with other girls she could insist on playing the part of the villain—a dangerous and devious man. Here a deeper gender identity could find acceptable expression.

But the arrival of puberty often dashes these early hopes. The transgender adolescent, longing to be known and accepted as a boy, instead experiences developing breasts and the onset of menstruation. Another transgender teenager, hoping to be transformed into a beautiful girl, instead faces the growth of facial hair, along with troubling erections. The emergence of these secondary sex characteristics brings a transformation, but not the one for which each had so earnestly hoped. Having been born "in the wrong body," they experience this untrustworthy body as betraying them yet again. Looking back, one trans man recalls his own experience: "Seeing my breasts and my period, I had nothing tangible to prove that I was male."

Most adolescents are intensely aware of their body and its perceived inadequacies. For transgender teenagers this sensitivity is much more intense. A fourteen-year-old adolescent—convinced that he is, in fact, a girl—will be extremely uncomfortable standing naked in a locker room with a group of boys. A transgender teenager raised as a girl may devote considerable effort to adopt the feminine role at home and at school, even though this playacting brings no delight and is not guided by internal gender clues.

As transgender youths look toward their future, sports and the military are often seen as arenas that would help them confirm their "correct" gender. Dawn describes her effort to succeed as a high school athlete and prove herself a man.

> I began high school and earned a starting position on the junior varsity football team. Suddenly I became part of the in-crowd, a jock ... by the time I graduated I had earned letters in football, track and tennis. At the Air Force Academy (all male then) I excelled again, playing football, soccer, rugby, as well as earning academic honors. I should have been happy but I wasn't (communication to authors).

The authors of *True Selves* observe, "Military training is a popular choice for both male and female transsexuals because it gives them not only a place to belong but also a strong sense of affiliation. For transgender females, it is one setting in which they are not only allowed to express a tougher, more masculine side of their nature but *expected* to do so." At the same time, "many transgender males join the military because they think it might make them more masculine"—and thus help them overcome their feminine self-awareness.

The Gendered Brain

The human brain, bathed in hormones that shape the individual's gender identity, "is a gendered organ, and gender identity is not a conscious decision. People do not choose to feel like a boy or a girl, or like both, or like neither. They simply are who they are. From this perspective, transgender people and all people whose gender identity does not align with their anatomical sex are simply *born that way*" (Brill and Pepper, *The Transgender Child*). Parents, then, are not to blame for their child's sense of gender identity. "If a professional tells you that you can change your child to have a different gender identity, they are wrong. There is nothing anyone can do to change a child's gender identity. It is a core part of self."

Developmental psychologist Diane Ehrensaft suggests that "gender is an interweaving of nature and nurture." Gender is not simply and definitively "dictated by our chromosomes, hormone receptors, or genitalia but by our own internal sense of self, a self that is influenced by biology, by rearing, and by culture." The complex reality that we call gender is composed of many elements. "A child's gender journey launched at birth is based on (1) *genetic gender*: chromosomal inheritance, be it XX, XY, or other; (2) *physical gender*: primary and secondary sexual characteristics—penis and testicles, or a vagina, ovaries, and uterus; and (3) *brain gender*, or functional structures of the brain along gender lines."

These distinctions allow us to recognize the differences between *gender identity* (the deep inner sense of gender, regardless of anatomy) and *gender expression*. "In contrast to gender identity, which is an internal feeling, gender expression is how we externalize our gender. It encompasses everything that communicates our gender to others: clothing, hairstyles, mannerisms, how we speak, how we play, and our social interaction and roles."

Stages of Development

Psychologists suggest that "gender identity emerges by age two to three and is influenced by biology and sociological factors." Psychologists point to the social cues that support this precocious awareness. "Parents talk differently to a male infant and a female infant; they hold baby girls longer; they encourage baby boys to strive to do things more. They dress their infants differently. In all these ways they mirror to the infant the child's gender identity" (Brill and Pepper).

By ages three to four, children have a sense of their own gender identity and are increasingly aware of anatomical differences. During these years a child might tell the parent, "I wish I was a boy," or announce, "My heart is boy, but my body is girl." Between ages four and six, children associate gender with specific behaviors: they become conscious of clothing and makeup; they pay attention to gender-specific toys, such as trucks or dolls. Between ages five and seven, children become aware that gender does not change; it is part of one's stable identity. Psychologists report that most trans children recognize the gender discrepancy by the time they begin school.

Between ages nine and twelve, a child's gender identity continues to stabilize. Many children who had earlier experimented with cross-gender behavior (a boy playing with dolls or a girl insisting on wearing male clothes) will now abandon these activities. But for the transgender child, the specter of puberty is likely to provoke increasing psychological distress.

With the onset of puberty, the transgender child's conviction—that his or her gender is different from the evidence on display in the genitals—comes under dramatic attack. At the prospect of the changes that accompany puberty, trans children often become depressed. They fear these changes, which would seem to condemn them for life to the "wrong gender." Melissa recalls her own panic:

> As my body began to change, it got further and further away from where I wanted it, and more importantly, where I felt it needed to be ... I felt more and more distant from other boys my age, even though I was becoming a man, just like them. My feelings ... often overwhelmed

me. No matter what I did, I could not stop or get rid of
this growing sensation (communication to authors).

Brill and Pepper judge, "There is no rule of thumb for when a cross-
gender child should be allowed to transition. But there usually comes a
time when your child's suffering is so obvious that, despite your concerns,
it is critically important to allow them to live in the world as they wish."
The authors add, "[W]hat is clear is that children who receive the support
of their families have the best outcomes in terms of their future health
and well-being." Some families, often with the support of psychological
counseling, come to a shared decision for the child to receive hormone
blockers that forestall puberty. This strategy gives the child—and the
family—time to further assess their commitment to the far-reaching
changes involved in gender confirmation.

Hormone blockers prevent the changes in facial and body bone
structure, muscle tone, and voice pitch that typically accompany puberty.
If desired, the teenager may take a further step, beginning a regime of
cross-sex hormones. Cross-sex hormones, which begin to conform the
physical body to the person's inner sense of self, can have serious side
effects. Later, gender-confirmation surgery will be another option for the
transgender young adult.

Schools and Bathrooms

Six-year-old Coy Mathis was born biologically a boy but had identified
as female for several years by the time she began kindergarten in the
Fountain-Fort Carson School District in Colorado. The school initially
responded positively to her parents' wish that she be allowed to use the
girls' bathroom at the school. After parents of a number of other children
complained, school administrators instructed Coy that she was to use the
gender-neutral bathroom in the school's health office.

Coy's parents sued the school district for violating their child's civil
rights. In June 2013, the state's civil rights division agreed that the school
had violated a Colorado antidiscrimination law that had, in 2008, been
extended to cover transgender persons. Steven Chavez, the division
director, wrote that telling this student that "she must disregard her
identity while performing one of the most essential human functions

constitutes severe and pervasive treatment, and creates an environment that is subjectively and objectively hostile, intimidating or offensive." Advocates for gender nondiscrimination hailed this judgment as setting a legal precedent in favor of transgender children and the use of gender-appropriate bathrooms. Today, more school systems are educating themselves about and showing more sensitivity toward gender-diverse children in their schools.

Joel Baum, executive director of Gender Spectrum, describes typical interventions by his organization to help prepare school administrators and teachers to welcome and support a student who was in the midst of gender transition. Their initiatives also included preparing the other children for this change as well as addressing immediate questions of clothing, sports participation, bullying, and restroom use.

In *The Transgender Child*, Brill and Pepper discuss challenges that families face at this time and report strategies that have proved helpful. Using bathroom facilities at school and other public settings can become traumatic for gender-variant children.

> For transgender children and teens, the bathroom can be a scary place that symbolizes their differentness. If your child is living in accordance with their gender identity, they may be especially afraid they will be found out in the bathroom. If they identify as transgender and are not yet living in accordance with their gender identity, they can feel like an imposter in the bathroom.

These authors encourage parents to have a realistic discussion with their child about the options and the dangers surrounding use of public bathrooms.

It's Not about Sexual Orientation

"Biological sex and gender are different ... Sexual orientation and gender identity are separate, distinct parts of a person's identity. Although your child may not yet be aware of their sexual orientation, they usually have a strong sense of their gender identity" (Brill and Pepper). Sexual orientation refers to those to whom I am romantically and physically attracted; gender identity refers to my deepest sense of *who I am* as a woman or a man. But this distinction can be confusing for a young transgender person. A teenager experiencing fluid or ambiguous gender awareness—for example, a female body in conflict with a deeper masculine identity—realizes that she does not fit the social description of a heterosexual woman: that is, a woman who is attracted to men. But she knows that there is an identifiable group of women—lesbians—who are attracted to other women. So she may conclude, "I must be a lesbian." Another transgender teenager is eager to date, as are most young people at this age. But this gender-variant boy has no desire to date girls; he insists, instead, that *he is a girl*! As the gay culture becomes more acceptable in school settings, identifying as gay may appeal to a transgender boy; this is a place to belong. But developing a close relationship with a gay friend is not likely to be satisfying. His gay friend relates to him as another boy, while he perceives himself as a girl and yearns to be liked and loved in this deeper identity—as a girl.

David describes the temporary comfort of living as a lesbian until he was able to confront the issue of being transgender. "I took refuge in a lesbian identity for a total of twenty-five years. There, I could wear my gender how it pleased me, as gay people in general tend to have a greater tolerance for a wide range of gender expressions, but not always for stated gender identities, at least not at that time. Most discussions of my nebulous gender identity ended in argument, so I learned to engage in this topic sparingly. I made friends and lived in a community I was mostly comfortable in. I got by."

Recent research highlights an encouraging generational change. Two-thirds of transgender members of the younger generation (eighteen- to twenty-four-year-olds in this research) were familiar with other trans persons in their own generation. Among those in midlife, many fewer knew of other transgender persons as they faced their early struggle of self-acceptance. The authors of the research are heartened by the accounts of these younger transgender men, "who are able to bypass those years of internal struggle and find their path more directly" (Beemyn and Rankin). They conclude, "[I]t is also exciting to realize that we are on the brink of a world in which transgender children and youth can be embraced and supported for who they are." This is a new and hopeful era.

Religious Questions

A religiously sensitive child or adolescent, struggling with gender identity, may lament, "Why did God make me this way?" Troubled parents, hoping to convince the child to turn away from these deviant feelings, may insist, "God does not make mistakes." This naïve judgment is meant to trump the young person's insistent testimony to personal identity. Here an anxious parent is pleading, "This can't be happening. The God I believe in would not allow such a thing!" The message the child receives is clear: "Please, please stop behaving this way!"

Parents who are more attentive to their child's development might also respond, "God does not make mistakes." But here the response would carry a very different message: "God has made you like this, my lovely and beloved child. And we, your family, will support you to live out your deepest identity in the way that is meaningful for you."

Yet too often religious leaders warn transgender children and young adults that they are in danger of being damned. Within the transgender community, this frequently offered punitive judgment has been called "the rape of the soul." Here religious faith becomes twisted to destructive purposes.

Born Intersex

A number of children, born in grace, are also born intersex—with ambiguous genitalia. *Intersex* identifies those whose bodies carry physical, hormonal, or chromosomal elements of both sexes. This condition may or may not be readily apparent at birth. Brill and Pepper offer this definition: "The term intersex refers to persons born with less than clearly defined, or some combination of, external genitalia or internal sexual organs." They explain: "Intersex babies are sometimes arbitrarily assigned a sex and gender at birth, based often on a single medical opinion, and surgeries have been performed to more clearly align a baby's genitalia to match a typical female or male child's anatomy." Brown and Rounsley provide this description: "Intersexed individuals ... are born with both ovarian and testicular tissue (either fully or partially developed). Some also have some obvious physical abnormality or ambiguity at the time of birth involving the external sex organs." Broadened understanding of this biological and genetic phenomenon now supports a more humane response to this reality, which is so bewildering for parents.

Amy Bloom estimates that about two thousand children with ambiguous genitals are born in the United States each year; this exceeds the annual number of infants born with cystic fibrosis. Many physical ambiguities are obvious at birth: testes that have not descended, an enlarged clitoris, an extremely small penis, a vagina not yet fully formed. But the intersex condition may not be discovered until later. For example, a child appears at birth as female; only subsequent physical examination of her groin reveals the absence of both uterus and fallopian tubes.

In the past, an infant with a very small penis or an overly large clitoris raised alarms for physicians and parents. The common medical practice was immediately to undertake surgery to "correct" the anomaly. For some births in hospital settings, these procedures were undertaken without parental knowledge or consent. Today the medical and psychological professions recognize that anomalous genitals do not necessarily lead to adult trauma. Bloom writes movingly of a man, now married with children, who despite being born with an extremely small penis escaped the knife of anxious surgeons. He now speaks publicly about the intersex experience, often telling an audience, "You may look at my penis and think it is pathetic; or you may look at it, as my wife and I do, and find it adorable."

Bloom describes the work of Cheryl Chase, founder of the Intersex Society of North America (ISNA). Chase, who was subjected to multiple surgeries to "correct" her genital self, is an active advocate for resisting the surgical intervention shortly after the birth of a child with ambiguous genitals. Bloom also interviewed Philip Gruppuso, professor of pediatrics and biochemistry at Brown University. Dr. Gruppuso criticizes the earlier approach of aggressive surgery and is concerned about "doctors being too sure of themselves, imagining that they control the outcome for sexual orientation and gender identity, and then doing irreversible surgery." He suggests that homophobia continues as an unacknowledged bias affecting medical response to infants with ambiguous genitals.

Caster Semenya is a world-class athlete. Born in South Africa, she gained international attention by winning the eight-hundred-meter race in the 2009 world championships. Her competitors, impressed both by her speed and her well-developed body, contested her gender status. Upon examination, it was discovered that Caster had internal testes instead of a uterus and ovaries, as well as a testosterone level three times that of the typical genetic female. Medical experts have made it clear that testosterone levels vary greatly in both women and men, making this an unreliable criterion for determining gender. Caster has now been certified by the International Association of Athletics Federations to compete internationally as a woman. Commenting on this humiliating public scrutiny, she simply remarks, "God made me the way I am, and I accept myself" (see Andrew Solomon's *Far from the Tree*).

Another group of individuals who do not fit the stereotype of male or female are those who are born genetically male (with XY chromosomes), but whose system is unable to take up their testosterone in developing a penis and other male body parts. A person with complete *androgen insensitivity syndrome* (AIS) appears to be female but has no uterus; at puberty breasts develop, but the individual does not menstruate. Complete *androgen insensitivity syndrome* is rarely discovered in childhood. Most persons with this condition are diagnosed only when they fail to get a menstrual period or have trouble getting pregnant. Treatment and gender assignment are a very complex issue and must be addressed for each person.

These two examples remind us that simplistic notions of "male and female God created them" need to be enriched by contemporary experience.

The Intersex Child: Calliope Becomes Cal

In 2003, Jeffrey Eugenides was awarded the Pulitzer Prize for his novel *Middlesex,* a *coming of age* story with a significant twist. The author recounts the fictional account of Calliope, a young girl growing up in the Detroit suburb of Middlesex. Reaching puberty, Calliope recognizes that that her sense of gender, as well as her body, is undergoing a transformation. Noticing the appearance of facial hair, her voice shifting lower, her (still) flat chest, and her new sexual interest in other girls, Calliope begins the traumatic gender transition to become the young man Cal.

Calliope has been raised as a girl. She was born with what appeared to be a vagina, though her vaginal pouch is not linked to a functioning uterus or ovaries. As a child, she is not troubled by her large clitoris. But with the release of testosterone at the time of puberty, her body begins the transition from "more girl-like" to "more boy-like."

Finally aware of her anomalous state, Calliope's parents bring her to an endocrinologist. Informed of the physician's plan to surgically relieve her of her enlarged clitoris and infuse her with hormones that would accentuate her female properties, Calliope goes to the library to learn more about her condition. In the large Webster dictionary she finds the definition of *hermaphrodite*—"one having the sex organs and many of the secondary sex characteristics of both male and female." The dictionary entry ended with the recommendation "see synonyms at *monster.*"

Rather than submit to surgery at age fourteen, Calliope leaves home for California. She cuts her long hair, buys male clothes, and practices walking like a man. Living now as *Cal,* this teenager slowly grows into a new gender identity. As the novel moves toward its conclusion, Cal returns to his family in the Midwest. There he found that for his family gender was not all that important. It seemed that the change from girl to boy was far less dramatic than the distance that all children travel from infancy to adulthood. Cal remained the same person, if now presenting as a male. "Even now, as I live as a man, I remain in essential ways Tessie's daughter. I'm still the one who remembers to call her every Sunday." The novel's moral point is clear: gender is not all that important—unless we make it so.

Conclusion

> *No part of the body may say of another, "I have no need of you."* —1 Corinthians 12:21

The New Testament has earned a bad reputation for introducing the stark opposition of flesh and spirit into Christian belief. "The spirit indeed is willing, but the flesh is weak" (Matthew 26:41). "Nothing good dwells within me, that is, in my flesh" (Romans 7:18). John's Gospel, written decades later, added fuel to the fire: "It is the spirit that gives life; the flesh is useless" (John 6:63). For many Christians, this seemed to endorse a suspicion of the body with its passionate fleshly stirrings. Does the spiritual life necessarily involve distrusting the body?

St. Paul redeemed himself—to some degree—with the evocative

metaphor of the Christian community as the body of Christ. "Now you are the body of Christ and individually members of it" (1 Corinthians 12:27). This metaphor asks Christians to frame their shared life as an organic reality with many diverse elements. Paul's metaphor insists on a certain democracy among these distinct members. Since all the members belong equally to the whole and are necessary for its coordinated life, no part of the body can say of another, "We do not need you."

Paul's imagery recognizes another distinctive feature of our frail human bodies, personal and communal. "Those members of the body that we think less honorable we clothe with greater honor, and our less respectable members are treated with greater respect" (v. 23). These parts—less respectable according to society's judgment and therefore more vulnerable—are to be cared for with great respect. Paul advances his thought, bringing together the equality and the vulnerability of the common body: "[I]f one member suffers, all members suffer together with it; if one member is honored, all rejoice with it" (v. 26).

Earlier in this letter, Paul has celebrated the variety of spiritual gifts evident among the body of believers. Each of these gifts has a contribution to make to the building up of the whole. Since all are essential to the community's well-being, none is to be turned away. As church groups and religious institutions offer more gracious welcome to the gender-diverse in our midst, we will be enriched by now-unrecognized gifts of the transgender children and adults among us.

Additional Resources

In *Gender Born, Gender Made*, Diane Ehrensaft focuses on effective care for transgender children and their families. Also see Stephanie Brill and Rachel Pepper, *The Transgender Child*, and Genny Beemyn and Susan Rankin, *The Lives of Transgender People*.

Amy Bloom discusses the intersex condition in *Normal: Transsexual CEOs, Cross-Dressing Cops, and Hermaphrodites with Attitude*. Alexander Hemon offers a profile of Lana Wachowski in "Beyond the Matrix," in the *New Yorker* (September 10, 2012). Wachowski's acceptance speech at the Human Rights Campaign award ceremony in 2013 is available on YouTube.

Dan Frosch reports on Coy Mathis and the Colorado school system in "Rights Unit Finds Bias against Transgender Student," the *New York Times* (June 24, 2013), and "Dispute on Transgender Rights Unfolds at a Colorado School," the *New York Times* (March 18, 2013).

Joel Baum is director of education and training at Gender Spectrum. This organization assists parents with gender-variant children to become more confident in caring for their child, who is negotiating the persistent desire to be recognized—and to dress as—the gender not assigned at birth. See www.genderspectrum.org.

The Center for Lesbian and Gay Studies, at the Pacific School of Religion, in Berkeley, California, sponsors a yearly gathering of families of transgender children. Educational sessions and support groups come together at this Transgender Religious Leaders Summit. The center's website is www.clgs.org. Also see the Family Acceptance Project: http://familyproject.sfsu.edu/.

For further discussion of intersex, see the Accord Alliance, formerly The Intersex Society of North America.

Chapter Fourteen

Transgender Lives Made Visible

Then the righteous will answer him, "Lord, when was it that we saw you hungry and gave you food ... saw you a stranger and welcomed you ... saw you sick or in prison and visited you?" —Matthew 25:39

Transgender lives remain invisible to most Americans. Throughout history, different social groupings have been assigned to the boundaries of society where they remain largely out of sight. In the novel *Invisible Man*, Ralph Ellison uses this metaphor to capture the cultural status of African Americans in midcentury America. Gays and lesbians remained for many decades in concealment—in darkened closets or segregated colonies—until the events at Stonewall in 1969 propelled them into full view. Erin Swenson, a transgender Presbyterian minister, remarks that "the transgendered in our congregations are invisible and will remain invisible until it is clear that they are accepted." Recent dramatic changes in American society have ushered the transgender community into the healing light.

The Shape of Invisibility

Many transgender adults report that early in life there were no names to describe the "disconnect" they experienced between their private sense of gender identity (who I am) and their bodily self (who I appear to be). They could recognize no one else as "like me." No one in the immediate environment reflected back to them a similar identity, affirming "I too am like this; I too have these feelings." Transgender persons were invisible both in society and to themselves.

Self-recognition is a critical element in what Erik Erikson describes as an initial stage of adult maturing: identity. The effort to forge an adult identity is not simply an interior task. The young adult looks to society for models, clues, and ideals. Having contact with a successful adult or inspiring role model, the younger person judges, "I could be like that. I would like to live that way."

Our personal identity is shaped in part by the exemplars of adult maturity that are available in our environment. For many transgender children and young adults, this resource is missing. In *The Lives of Transgender People*, Beemyn and Rankin describe this challenge of self-recognition: "Learning about or meeting other transgender people serves as a catalyst for self-recognition and acceptance, as they see themselves in others and realize that they are not alone in how they feel."

Deprived of persons who might affirm the shape of their own uncommon identity, young trans persons are often at a loss: Who am I? Where do I belong? What am I worth? Such recognition—begun in the parent's loving gaze early in infancy and then repeated in the many ways that adults affirm, reinforce, and praise a child for being his or her (gendered) self—is utterly absent. The trans youth feels not only disconnected but invisible, unable to find a place in an unfamiliar world. This is the making of craziness.

Today many trans youth report that they first recognized themselves on the Internet. But many older adults were not so fortunate: "[T]here were no resources—like the [I]nternet—which I could consult to help me cope with how I felt. I was very much alone with my 'dark secrets' and it was not until I went online in 1997 that I realized how un-alone I was" (Beemyn and Rankin). Here trans invisibility was erased, as individuals had access to information that spoke to their own experiences. Self-worth and self-confidence expanded as the sense of isolation began to lift: "I exist; I am real; I am okay."

Lives Made Visible: Living Witnesses

In the past decade, a new generation has given greater visibility to the transgender experience. Here we offer three distinguished examples, in the lives of a concert pianist, an Episcopal priest, and a university professor.

Sara Davis Buechner is a concert pianist and professor of music at the University of British Columbia. As David Buechner, she trained at Juilliard and subsequently won several awards at the world's most prestigious piano competitions. But after completing gender transition in 1998, Buechner experienced a dramatic falloff in her performance career. She writes, "[I]n the United States once I came out as Sara, I couldn't get bookings with the top orchestras anymore, nor would any university hire me. In Canada, the University of British Columbia in Vancouver hired me for a piano fellowship in 2003, and in 2008 I earned tenure." Today she regularly offers concerts throughout North America, Asia, and Europe, and she continues to teach at the University of British Columbia.

Cameron Partridge is an Episcopal priest who as a seminarian informed the bishop that he would be transitioning from female to male. The bishop responded, "I'm old enough now that when I feel discomfort that probably means God wants me to pay attention to this." After four years of conversation with his bishop, Partridge was ordained in 2005 and received a doctor of theology degree from Harvard in 2008. In his ministry as campus chaplain at Boston University, he has been able to counsel and accompany students and staff who have questions about gender identity.

Jennifer Finney Boylan is a successful novelist and popular professor of literature at Colby College in Maine. She began her transition from James to Jenny after teaching for twelve years at this institution. In her book *She's Not There: A Life in Two Genders*, Boylan describes her pretransition struggle with her transgender status in the metaphor of invisibility: "It was an absurdity I carried everywhere, a crushing burden, which was, simultaneously, invisible. Trying to make the best of things, trying to snap out of it, didn't help."

When she determined that her sanity demanded her gender transition, she spoke first to the college president and then to deans and key professors to prepare them for the transition. She then took a sabbatical, timed with the hormonal and surgery transition. Being well-known and appreciated at the university allowed for her smooth transition from James to Jenny. Boylan describes her transition: "The biggest change for me is not going from male to female; it's going from someone who has a secret to someone who doesn't really have secrets anymore."

Lives Made Visible: Societal Changes

In February 2013, the US Congress renewed the Violence against Women Act, a law that includes protection to all women, irrespective of sexual orientation or gender identity. By mid-2013, ten states and the District of Columbia were providing some form of legal protection for transgender people.

The American Psychiatric Association published the fifth edition of its professional standards, the *Diagnostic and Statistical Manual of Mental Disorders* (DSM-5) in March 2013. In this influential statement, the earlier diagnostic language that identified a transgender person as suffering from "gender identity disorder" was deleted, replaced by the designation of "gender dysphoria." The term *disorder* was judged to be inaccurate— even prejudicial, since it identified the transgender within the category of mental illness. *Dysphoria* honors the intense distress reported by some transgender persons, but it recognizes that this usually temporary experience represents neither a character disorder nor a mental illness. This authoritative action by the APA culminates a long process of testimony, debate, and conversion of health professionals. Its announcement stands as a watershed: decades of prejudice and discrimination are beginning to give way to a more nuanced understanding of human development.

Over many decades, college or university student health insurance plans offered no coverage for gender reassignment surgery. Stanford University began covering sex-reassignment surgery in 2010. In February 2013, Brown University announced that its student health plan would be extended to cover sex-change surgery, becoming the thirty-sixth college to do so. Twenty-five other colleges do not cover the expensive surgical procedures but have plans covering related hormone therapy; twenty universities provide similar coverage for their employees. Today about a quarter of Fortune 500 companies have health plans that cover similar medical and/or surgical procedures for employees.

Lives Made Visible: Welcoming Communities of Faith

Bertie Brouhard is a retired engineer in her sixties. A longtime member of the St. Mark's Lutheran Church in San Francisco, Bertie is an enthusiastic lector and a volunteer in the community's various outreach ministries. Three years ago, the person well-known in the congregation as Bob

Brouhard announced plans to begin the social and medical procedures of gender transition. This decision had come after much soul-searching and spiritual discernment. Initially the members of the staff were perplexed and discomforted, but they were determined to accompany Bertie through this transition. Returning to the congregation as Roberta, Bertie continued in her role as lector and active volunteer. She took advantage of the adult education hour that was part of the Sunday morning gathering, discussing this gender transition, which was a critical moment in her journey of faith. Many in the congregation were initially bewildered. But soon, and with some hesitance, they welcomed Bertie as the respected and well-loved person whom they had known earlier as Bob. Later that year, the congregation at St. Mark's participated in a renaming ceremony, during which Bertie was officially welcomed into the community in her new gender.

Stephanie Battaglino has been a corporate vice president at a major Fortune 100 life insurance company headquartered in New York for many years and is a vocal advocate for transgender rights. She transitioned in 2005, becoming the first transgender person to do so in the 165-year history of her company. In a speech to her Episcopal parish commemorating the 2012 Transgender Day of Remembrance, she thanked the community that had given her the friendship and compassion that allowed her to work through the challenges surrounding her transition. In this same speech she traced the Paschal dimensions of her transition: "If I stepped into it, I risked losing everything—my life as I knew it was over. But I did anyway, and I stand before you this morning as a testament to the fact that there is life after the abyss. I am sure God was present with me that day and days afterwards, but I was too caught up in all the other earthly things associated with my transition to stop and feel His embrace" (communication to authors).

Stephanie describes the focus of her current advocacy work: "I have worked in corporate America my entire career—I know the landscape and the politics of it well, so in discerning how best to be an advocate for my community, it was a logical place for me to begin my efforts to 'move the needle' with respect to transgender equality." Stephanie lives in New Jersey with her partner, Mari, and her son, Andrew.

Anakin Morris, baptized Anna Katherine Morris twenty-three years ago, is a personable young man working in a legal aid organization in Chicago. His is a story of exceptional good fortune and community support.

Throughout the high-school years and even earlier, Anna was aware that she was not like other girls. In the junior and senior years of high school, Anakin identified herself as a lesbian. Wearing her hair short and spiked, and adopting masculine clothing styles moved Anna away from a traditional feminine self-presentation. At this point, Anakin remembers, his only awareness of transgender came from the films *Boys Don't Cry* and *Rent*—where transgender provoked violence, even murder. This was not an identity to be sought.

Moving away from home to begin studying at a university, Anakin recalls several chance meetings on campus with students who openly identified themselves as transgender. At this point, something clicked: *this is who I am.* By the end of the first semester, Anakin became convinced that he could no longer understand himself as a lesbian; recognizing himself as male, he determined to begin the process of transition. By great good fortune, Anakin received strong support from his mother. With her he was able to discuss the bewildering changes—medical and social—that he was experiencing. She, in turn, began to prepare other family members for future development as Anna became Anakin.

In her first month at the university, Anna had volunteered to lead the youth religion classes at the university's Catholic Student Center. At the start of the winter quarter of freshman year Anna returned as Anakin. His close friends in the dorm who had followed his gender transition were supportive. The staff at the Catholic Center, impressed with the good response Anna had received from the participants in her religious education classes, welcomed Anakin to continue to serve in this program (communication to authors).

Bertie, Stephanie, and Anakin represent a new generation of transgender Christians. Supported by family and friends and communities of faith, they have successfully navigated a harrowing transition and discovered a hard-won freedom. Their experiences announce a new and hopeful era.

What Christian Communities Can Do

A family, embarrassed by a transgender child, falls into silence. Uncomfortable with what they understand to be the transgender experience, public and private organizations ignore or dismiss their concerns. More tragically, Christian pastors, ill-informed and defensive, resort to religious prejudices to threaten transgender members with social rejection, amid threats of eternal damnation. Erin Swenson, a transgender Presbyterian minister, laments the ignorance and neglect that describe many Christian communities today. "Professionals, including clergy, have contributed to shame-based avoidance [of transgender persons] through persistent ignorance and phobic reaction."

Yet in many places these strategies of silence and condemnation are giving way to more enlightened and compassionate responses. As the statement of the United Methodist Church's *Made in God's Image* observes, "We understand our gender diversity to be a gift of God, intended to add to the rich variety of human experience and perspective."

Swenson encourages faith communities to provide a welcoming place for trans persons. This openness is rooted in the countercultural recognition that transgender persons are today's equivalent of the social outcasts in ancient Israel. This memory arises from Psalm 82: "Give justice to the weak and orphan; maintain the right of the lowly and the destitute; rescue the weak and the needy." Swenson suggests that "pastors of larger or urban congregations may consider developing an adult course, reading or discussion group on gender issues, in which transgender experience is a topic ... The most compelling exposure to transgender experience comes in the encounter with real people who are struggling to live real lives." She adds, "[M]any transgender support groups struggle to find a safe and economical space for their meetings. Faith communities that are welcoming can make a strong statement of support for transgender experience by hosting and integrating such a group in the ministry of the community."

A colleague who has dedicated the last decade to ministering to transgender persons has created an educational format to bring faith communities to a greater awareness of their transgender members. In an event she names a Trans Awareness Evening, she invites people with open hearts and minds to a gathering to listen to the stories of several trans persons whom she has been accompanying on their spiritual journey. Participants are encouraged to ask questions and deepen their awareness of these members of the Christian body.

She offers further details of these events. "As the sessions evolved, the panelists included male to female transsexuals, female to male transsexuals, and the mother of a transsexual. The format remained the same—sharing of stories by the panelists, questions and discussion, and then a good bit of time to mingle and chat. Those attending were genuinely eager to learn and understand. They left with a great appreciation of some of God's children they previously knew nothing about and a desire to learn more and share with others what they had experienced. They had allowed the boundaries of their hearts to be stretched" (communication to authors).

Pastoral Responses of Welcome and Inclusion

Pastoral care for members of the trans community includes attitudes and programs found to be effective in (1) welcoming members of the trans community, (2) inviting their participation in parish life, (3) supporting their spiritual growth, and (4) providing services appropriate to the needs and interests of trans members and their families.

We begin at the personal level, examining ways that those in ministry can serve as an effective pastoral presence, helping faith communities welcome and witness to members of the trans community. For many of us, a necessary first step is to *learn* more. In order to be genuinely welcoming and supportive, we need to understand the issues that are significant to trans folks. But of equal importance is learning more about ourselves. Self-examination helps us recognize there is much we don't yet understand about the concerns and hopes of the trans community. Perhaps even more important, self-examination helps us confront our own convictions, prejudices, and hesitancies around the trans experience.

Valuable information is available from many sources. If we are fortunate, we can learn from trans persons who are already part of our interpersonal world—members of our own family or close friends or work colleagues. And we can seek information from other sources—parents of trans children, advocacy groups supportive of the trans community. Local civic groups and social service organizations are often eager to provide information. And public libraries can suggest reliable sources of information on the medical, legal, and social dimensions of the transgender experience.

Developing personal relationships with members of the trans community will be important in our efforts to include trans persons in the life of the church. The skills and convictions that generally help us to honor other people and put them at ease will serve us well in welcoming members of the trans community. Including trans persons in parish life does not require establishing new programs from the start. Many of the ordinary activities of a vital parish—communal worship, small prayer groups, fellowship activities, social outreach ministries—interest trans people as well.

In addition, there are particular needs that trans persons and their families experience, and ministries focused on these needs are appreciated. It is often transgender persons themselves who serve best in recommending and developing programs appropriate to the spiritual growth of members of the trans community. So be ready to ask trans people about their needs and interests and experiences, learning from them how the parish can be more inclusive.

Effective pastoral care for members of the trans community usually begins in personal contact, taking practical steps that let trans people know they are welcome. Effective welcome goes beyond just providing general information about parish life, to including more focused efforts inviting trans persons to participate in parish programs. Perhaps accompany trans persons to a meeting or recruit trans members to serve on committees or connect them with a task force where the particular talent or skill they bring will be especially helpful.

Our trans friends suggest that thoughtful people should not be shy about approaching trans persons with questions. They suggest that if someone has identified as trans to you, your relationship is probably strong enough for you to bring up sensitive questions. Most trans persons are eager to provide information, in ways that honor their lives and enable you to be more confident in dealing with the trans experience. And hearing the personal stories of members of the trans community is a powerful learning experience.

As awareness and sensitivity to the trans experience develop, prayer remains an essential resource. Prayer in gratitude for the ways in which members of the trans community have enriched our faith communities. Prayer for society's change of heart, moving toward a greater appreciation of the trans experience. Prayer for the leaders in our religious institutions, that compassion and justice may increasingly guide their response to transgender persons.

A Theological Reflection: Created in the Image of God

We believe that life in the Spirit links us with a mysterious, surprising, extravagant Creator. Fashioned out of dust, we are *"born in the image of God."* (Genesis 1:27) But what does this mean? It cannot be in our maleness or femaleness that we reflect God, since the Most High who is revealed to us in scripture is not gendered. But humans are born with capacities for love and compassion and justice; we possess the potential to be courageous and generous and forgiving. Surely these are the qualities that most reflect the image of God in us. The challenge today is to disengage our lives as reflections of God from the cultural constraints of gender. As we are able to do this, our eyes open to the extravagant diversity of creation.

"Male and female God made them" (Genesis 1:27). Again we might ask, What does this passage convey? Throughout Christian history interpreters have seen here a biblical warrant for a fixed binary order of gender ("two and only two"). Much theological discourse—and not a little confusion—has sprung from this interpretation of the would-be "natural order" of a gendered creation.

Coming from God, the created universe bears God's signature. Christian theologians early on sought to explain how creation or "nature" serves as a reflection of the Creator. The theological concept of the *natural law* arose from this impulse. This development has had a positive aspect: we recognize that we can glimpse something of God's design and beauty in the natural world—despite its brokenness and violence. But there have been negative consequences as well, as *human nature* has been dichotomized as male and female and *human fruitfulness* demoted to procreation.

This schema leaves little space for the extravagant paradoxes found throughout scripture. In the Hebrew Bible we meet Sarah, who is aged yet bears a child. At the beginning of the New Testament we encounter Mary, who is a virgin yet pregnant with a son. Both stories tell us that God's ways are not limited to biological forces; in human life, biology is not destiny. The revelation given in these events challenges a rigid view of human nature. The life of faith surpasses the bounds of the natural.

When we force our experience of humanity into stereotypical molds of male and female, we attempt a literal reading of reality that is at odds with our richly symbolic biblical heritage. In this effort we limit the biblical text to a single meaning. The dazzling extravagance of revelation throughout the Bible is frozen in one narrow reading of the text.

In a life of discipleship, as we follow the path of Jesus Christ, cultural differences and prejudices begin to fall away. We come to see that human nature is not simply a biologically determined essence; we recognize that our lives are not only about biological givens, but rather about what, in God's extravagant design, we might become. We become more capable of welcoming those who differ from us, even those whom society has rejected. In our support for transgender persons, compassion and justice embrace as we glimpse intimations of the coming reign of God.

Additional Resources

In her autobiographical reflection *Conundrum,* Jan Morris offers a moving memoir of her own transition. The film *TRANS* includes interviews with a variety of transgender persons; for viewing, see www.transthemovie.com.

Erin Swenson's reflections appear in "Pastoral Care in Transgender Experience," The Southern Association for Gender Education [SAGE] (Institute for Welcoming Resources, 2001). See Genny Beemyn and Susan Rankin, *The Lives of Transgender People.*

Becky Garrison discussed Cameron Partridge's journey in "Crossing Boundaries: A Transgender Priest Becomes a University Chaplain," a report published on January 3, 2013, by the John C. Danforth Center on Religion and Politics at Washington University in St. Louis.

A particularly helpful resource for discussion in religious groups is Ann Thompson Cook's *Made in God's Image: A Resource for Dialogue about the Church and Gender Differences,* a publication of Dumbarton United Methodist Church in Washington, DC.

Chapter Fifteen

The Prophetic Imagination: Sexuality and Justice

Faith is a living out of the figures of hope unleashed by the imagination. —Paul Ricoeur

Religious faith is a way of imagining the world. Recognizing that our existence is sustained by a loving Creator who is powerfully present yet beyond our ordinary power of sight requires a strong imagination. But this does not reduce faith to a fantasy or a mere figment of the mind. We appreciate faith—the ability to see the world in a particular and powerful way—as a gift. This blessing has been experienced across the generations. When our religious ancestors, having escaped slavery in Egypt, found themselves lost in the desert, some began to dream of "a land flowing with milk and honey." This ideal existed first only in their imaginations, fevered perhaps by the heat of the desert, but it was a hope that would become a reality.

The prophet Isaiah, troubled by the endless violence in his culture, imagined the possibility of another way of living. He pictured a world where "swords are beaten into plows" (Isaiah 2:4). This image rose against the evidence—then and now. The prospect of a more peaceful world existed first only in his imagination. But once expressed, this hope has galvanized generations of Jews and Christians. The world we inhabit today, with its arms industry and wars, does not support such fantasies. Yet peacemakers everywhere continue to be sustained by this dream, this hope, this way of imagining humanity's future. Walter Brueggemann defines biblical revelation as "an act of faithful imagination that buoyantly and defiantly mediates a counter-world that is a wondrous demanding alternative to the world immediately and visibly at hand."

Today we can appreciate more fully the role of imagination in the life of the spirit. Hope first stirs in the imagination, releasing us from the limitations imposed by present circumstances. Compassion arises as we are moved by the images of another's plight. Reinforced by the witness of biblical stories of hope and compassion, these fragile emotions mature into reliable virtues.

Imagination animated the spirituality of our religious ancestors. Ignatius Loyola, for example, began his own spiritual journey in response to interior illuminations. As John O'Malley writes in *The First Jesuits*, "by consulting his inner experience, [Ignatius] gradually came to the conviction that God was speaking to him through it, and he resolved to begin an entirely new life." And from the beginning, imagination has a central place in the *Spiritual Exercises* at the heart of Ignatian spirituality. The *Exercises* instruct us to start each meditation with a "composition of place"—bringing a Gospel story vividly to life. Holding this scene from Jesus's life in imagination gives focus and feeling to the meditation that follows.

This evidence from our spiritual heritage invites us to cultivate the imagination as a spiritual resource. Turning to the imagination, we are struck first by its volatility. Imagination sometimes harbors fantasies of violence and revenge. In its storehouse of painful memories obsessions can take hold. But imagination is more than a rogue faculty. Like our capacities for reasoning and feeling, imagination awaits cultivation. Well nurtured, the imagination can envision a world of peace and justice—and motivate us to pursue this dream. The religious heritage of prophecy stands as guarantee of this hope.

The Prophetic Imagination

In *The Prophetic Imagination*, Walter Brueggemann outlines the prophet's role both in ancient Israel and now. He stresses that prophets help a believing community *see through the present*, so that they may recognize God's action breaking into life. For Brueggemann, the *present* includes all the duties, delights, and distractions that fill our days. The present absorbs our attention: the good we are doing and the troubles we are avoiding conspire to consume all our energy. These daily duties, faithfully repeated, become the *status quo*. We are informed that "this is how we do it around here," and soon we come to accept that "this is the only way to do things." In time we may even come to believe that our customary way of proceeding is "God's eternal will for us." Brueggemann deploys the ominous phrase *the royal arrangement* to describe the status quo when it has become identified as God's will. Whether in ancient Israel or contemporary life, religious leaders are tempted to identify the current way of doing things with God's unchanging plan for humankind. Gradually then God's surprising presence is replaced by predictable patterns and unchangeable institutional procedures. Challenging these royal arrangements, "the vocation of the prophet was to keep alive the ministry of the imagination, to keep on conjuring and proposing alternative futures."

Prophets help a religious community see through the present by asking a provocative question: *What time is it?* Royal arrangements, whether sponsored by kings or bishops, reinforce an orthodoxy that hopes to escape the winds of time. The prophet Jeremiah, grieved by Israel's neglect of the poor and the outcast, warned the people that it was time to change their ways: "Even the stork in the heavens knows its times; and the turtledove, swallow, and crane observe the time of their coming; but my people do not know the ordinance of the Lord" (Jeremiah 8:7). Refusing to recognize what time it was, the people ignored the prophet's warning. And soon the time arrived when they were driven into exile, to wear the yoke of prisoners in a foreign land.

A generation later, the prophet Isaiah challenged the people's despair as they survived as strangers in a foreign land. Now is the time, he announced, for God to lead them back to their homeland. To this disheartened people the prophet spoke words of the Lord: "I am about to do a new thing; now it springs forth, do you not perceive it?" (Isaiah 43:19).

The Bible Tutors the Imagination

How are we to recognize the *new thing* that Isaiah proclaimed? Theologian William Spohn has explored the role of scripture in shaping the religious imagination. He reminds us that the Bible does not tell us directly what to do in every circumstance of our lives. Instead its stories and symbols "encourage certain scenarios." These stories—Jesus's welcoming openness toward sinners, his insistence we be prepared to forgive "seventy times seven," his compassion in healing the sick "become scenarios for action by evoking affective energies in distinctive ways." Faith stirs as we turn to these biblical accounts again and again, bathing our imaginations to this vision of reality. Through its dramatic parables and compelling images, the Bible serves to "tutor the imagination."

This biblical formation invites us to recognize that these "others"— outsiders, foreigners, all those who make us uncomfortable—are included in the family of God. This recognition requires a well-cultivated imagination. Two scriptural themes in particular shape our imaginations toward generosity and justice.

"You shall not oppress a resident alien; you know the heart of an alien for you were aliens in the land of Egypt" (Exodus 23:9). The Jews, once settled in their homeland, retained searing memories of slavery in Egypt and later exile in Babylon. Even in their freedom, the Israelites struggled to preserve their religious identity among a host of tribes with different gods and alien practices. Here Yahweh instructs them to respect and care for others now suffering the displacement they had once endured: "You must not molest the stranger or oppress him, for you lived as strangers in the land of Egypt" (Exodus 22:21; Jerusalem Bible translation). Scripture's repeated call to protect the outsider, the stranger, and the immigrant speaks to contemporary experience across the world.

As we bathe our imaginations in this biblical concern for a just treatment of foreigners and outsiders, we sense a resonance with the plight of immigrants in the United States today. Many Americans— including Christians—reject these "intruders" who have illegally entered our land and now threaten our scarce resources. Resentful of newcomers, we conveniently forget that not many generations ago our own ancestors arrived as strangers, seeking freedom and opportunity in this new place.

In another Gospel account, we read Jesus's surprising response to those who informed him that his mother and brothers had just arrived. "Who is my mother and my brothers?" he asks rather curtly (Mark 3:33). With this unsettling remark, Jesus questions the bounds of belonging— the bloodlines that are so essential to social life; the heritage of clan and tribe that define who belongs and who does not. He suggests a radically different way to imagine family: "Whoever does the will of God is my brother and my sister and my mother" (v. 35). This is an abrupt redrawing of the lines of family. If the appearance of outsiders in our society causes concern, questioning family boundaries generates an even higher alert. Yet the Gospels offer us a more capacious vision. Jesus's family encompasses all those who, themselves blessed by the grace of God, respond to the call for hospitality and justice. Uncomfortable insights ensue: gay and lesbian believers are to be welcomed into the Christian family; transgender persons are to be acknowledged as family. The prophetic imagination supports this more inclusive embrace of the family of God.

Reimagining the Stranger

Strangers appear throughout the Bible as vehicles of revelation. The crucial call to Abraham at the dawn of the biblical story is announced through the appearance of "three strangers" (Genesis 18). Later, Jacob wrestles in the dark with an unknown opponent who, by daylight, he will recognize as his God (Genesis 32). The message is repeated and clear: God often comes to us through strangers.

The book of Ruth includes another poignant story. Ruth is a triple outsider: she is a foreigner; she is a woman; she is a childless widow. By the alchemy of God's graciousness, this vulnerable stranger becomes the ancestor of "our kind." Her child is the grandfather of David, whose lineage culminates in the birth of Jesus.

This attention to outsiders continues in the parables of the New Testament. Near the end of Matthew's Gospel we learn of the significance that God assigns to compassion for the *other*. When the end of time arrives, Jesus insists, we will be judged according to our care for the vulnerable. "At that time the Lord will say to the just:

> I was hungry and you gave me food, I was thirsty and you gave me something to drink, I was a stranger and you welcomed me, I was naked and you gave me clothing, I was sick and you took care of me, I was in prison and you visited me (Matthew 25:35).

But those in Jesus's audience were befuddled by these words. They asked, "When did we see the Lord hungry or thirsty or naked?" The surprising response: when we extend our compassion to a stranger—"the least of the brethren"—it is Jesus himself whom we serve. Matthew's Gospel echoes God's demand in the book of Isaiah, that we turn away from the pious displays of fasting and spend our effort in justice toward the lowly. "Such fasting as you do today will not make your voice heard on high ... is this not the fast that I choose: to loose the bonds of injustice ... is it not to share your bread with the hungry, and bring the homeless poor into your house; when you see the naked to clothe them?" (Isaiah 58: 4; 6–7).

The most dramatic New Testament story about the stranger appears toward the end of Luke's Gospel. Two disciples are trudging home to the city of Emmaus, grief-stricken after the death of Jesus. They are joined by someone they do not recognize. This stranger questions them about their distress and then reminds them of the prophets' teaching that we come to life through death. Reaching their home, the disciples invite the stranger to join them for dinner. And in the breaking of the bread they recognize the stranger as Christ. Then, curiously, Jesus immediately disappears. The recognition has come in a flash—a sudden epiphany. The Lord's disappearance is not a cause of grief or distress for the two disciples. Instead they acknowledge, "[W]ere not our hearts burning within us!" (Luke 24:32). The story of Emmaus moves us today because our imaginations have been shaped by this story. In blessed moments, we have recognized in the stranger or vulnerable outsider, the face of Christ.

Whatever Happened to the Prophetic Imagination?

For nearly a thousand years the ministry of prophecy flourished in ancient Israel. From Nathan in the time of David, to Daniel eight centuries later, prophets raised unsettling questions that called the community to renewed fidelity. Jesus continued in this line of prophets, announcing a mysterious reign of God emerging in his own time. Historians tell us that for two centuries after the time of Jesus, the ministry of prophecy continued within Christian communities. But at some point in the early third century, this ministerial calling seems to have disappeared.

During this same historical period, Christian leaders were establishing the canon of scripture: which of the many documents circulating in Christian communities would be deemed as essential. A consensus emerged that sacred revelation was now accomplished: God had made available all that was needed for salvation. In these circumstances, perhaps prophecy was no longer needed. If the work of divine revelation is complete, then human imagination could serve only as a troublesome faculty, generating images and dreams that could prove unorthodox, even heretical.

Over the following centuries prophets were often seen as exotic figures, persons with the magical ability to see many years into the future. Today prophecy is less often seen as an exotic gift of predicting the future, but more often as the daring ability to see through the limits of the present. And today we find prophets among us again—Nelson Mandela, Dorothy Day, Martin Luther King Jr. But in many places, the church has yet to recover this once potent contribution to the community of faith.

Seeing Through the Present: Two Contemporary Voices

Philosopher Roberto Unger approaches the challenges of an institution seeking to *see through the present* with an insightful distinction. Much of the work of an institution, like the Catholic Church, is undertaken *within the framework* of the organization—an arrangement that we take for granted. In such an institutional structure, many established policies go unchallenged or even unnoticed. But on occasion, questions arise *about the organizational framework itself.* Such questions often provoke an institutional crisis. Unger recognizes that "only when there is a crisis— that is to say, a problem for which the established structure offers no ready-made solution—do we hit against the limits of our present ideas and methods." It is at such a point—an impasse—that an organization may be open to the prophetic imagination.

In a time of great cultural change, an institution must "be able to make moves it never made before, according to rules it can formulate, if at all, only after making them." This prospect can be terrifying for an institution that is wedded to historical precedent, but it is crucial for survival in the face of social upheaval. Unger notes that at such critical moments in an organization's life, imagination works like "a scout of the will," suggesting creative strategies for getting from here (an impasse) to a better place. An institution such as the church need not wait for a severe crisis to force reform. "The imagination does the work of crisis without crisis, making it possible for us to experience change without undergoing ruin."

Theologian Bradford Hinze identifies a mood of dismay and disappointment that runs through the Catholic Church today. He points to the continuing clergy sexual abuse scandal; the rollback of Vatican II reforms in liturgy; the intransigent resistance of bishops to accepting women in leadership roles; the demeaning treatment of gay and lesbian members of the church as instances of the church at an impasse. Confronting an impasse, a group becomes disoriented—unable to move forward or backward. Here the usual resources of rational analysis and strategic planning seem to abandon us. But this disorienting experience sometimes carries hidden opportunity. Such an impasse may serve as "a crucible for desire, reason, memory and imagination."

Acknowledging the impasse confronting the church today, Hinze draws attention to the biblical tradition of lamentation. As believers in ancient Israel grieved their losses, Catholics today experience regret and sorrow in response to a troubled institution. Hinze urges the body of the faithful to "create a public space for the people of God—not just the descendants of the apostles, martyrs, and ascetics, but all the faithful—to speak up for themselves and voice their own laments." He calls for "a pastoral communal process for personal and communal laments to be articulated and heard in synods, dioceses, and parishes." In such honest conversations, often filled with regret and lament, we may find our way through this impasse to a renewed community of faith.

The impasse that blocks the church's vitality today often centers on questions of sexuality and gender. Ecclesial leaders deny that women can possess the skills and gifts of priestly leadership. The institution confronts an impasse in regard to same-gender marriage: How can a couple who cannot biologically reproduce create a life together that is fruitful? And the experience of its transgender members is equally confounding: How can a factor as essential to human nature as *male* and *female* be questioned and perhaps reunderstood? In regard to each of these experiences the institutional church is in crisis. And yet many Christians today, their imaginations shaped by biblical convictions, see immigrants, homosexuals, and transgender persons in a new light. The virtue of hope strengthens these believers "in the meantime" as they pray with confidence that the institutional church will find its way through these impasses. This hope is rooted in the power of biblical stories to tutor our imaginations in the ways of mercy and justice.

The Imagination and the Reign of God

> *The discipline of reality is nothing without the grace of imagination.* —Ricoeur

Jesus, continuing in the line of prophets, began his ministry with this declaration: "[T]he time is fulfilled; and the reign of God has come near. Repent and believe in the good news" (Mark 1:15). Later he insisted to his listeners, "[T]he reign of God is already among you" (Luke 17:21). Jesus the prophet saw through the present to the in-breaking of a new and different time. He saw, in imagination, what his disciples could not yet envision.

The kingdom of God exists first in our hopeful imagination. This enduring hope anchors every effort of justice and mercy. The reign of God, alive in our imaginations, is both *already* and *not yet*. Each time a community of faith welcomes an "apparent outsider" and extends hospitality to those who have been marginalized, the reign of God comes closer to reality. This biblical ideal becomes more visible and believable. Each time a community shuts its heart to those judged to be unworthy members of the family, this hope recedes from view, appearing like little more than a pious fantasy. So the reign of God expands and contracts; we glimpse its graceful appearance, and then we lose sight of it once again. But we are buoyed by knowing that although our best efforts of justice and mercy are essential to this great ambition, the coming of the reign of God is finally the work of God's Spirit.

Additional Resources

Walter Brueggemann defines biblical faith in *The Prophetic Imagination*. Also see his "imaginative remembering" in *An Introduction to the Old Testament*. See John O'Malley's discussion of Ignatius's reliance on his interior experience and the "illuminations" produced by his imagination in *The First Jesuits*.

Roberto Unger explores the challenge of an institution to not simply repeat itself in *The Self Awakened*. Bradford Hinze explores impasses in the life of the church in "Ecclesial Impasse: What Can We Learn from Our Laments?" in *Theological Studies*. He borrows the linkage of impasse and lamentation from Constance Fitzgerald's essay "Impasse and Dark Night," in *Women's Spirituality*.

See William Spohn, "Jesus and Christian Ethics," in *Theological Studies*.

Bibliography

Beemyn, Genny, and Susan Rankin. *The Lives of Transgender People.* New York: Columbia University Press, 2011.

Benedict XVI. *God Is Love (Deus Caritas Est).* www.vatican.va.

Bloom, Amy. *Normal: Transsexual CEOs, Cross-Dressing Cops, and Hermaphrodites with Attitude.* New York: Random House, 2002.

Boylan, Jennifer Finney. *She's Not There: A Life in Two Genders.* New York: Broadway Books, 2003.

Bowlby, John. *A Secure Base: Parent-Child Attachment and Healthy Human Development.* New York: Basic Books, 1988.

———. *Becoming Attached: First Relationships and How They Shape Our Capacity to Love.* New York: Oxford University Press, 1991.

Brown, Brene. *Daring Greatly: How the Courage to be Vulnerable Transforms the Way We Live, Love, Parent and Lead.* New York: Gotham, 2012.

———. *The Power of Vulnerability: Teachings on Authenticity, Connection and Courage.* New York: Gotham, 2012.

Brown, M., and C. A. Rounsley. *True Selves: Understanding Transsexualism.* San Francisco: Jossey-Bass, 1996.

Brown, Peter. *Augustine of Hippo: A Biography.* Berkeley: University of California Press, 1967.

———. *Body and Society: Men, Women and Sexual Renunciation in Early Christianity.* New York: Columbia University Press, 1988.

Brueggemann, Walter. *An Introduction to the Old Testament.* Louisville: Westminster John Knox, 2003.

———. *The Prophetic Imagination.* Philadelphia: Fortress Press, 1978.

Buechner, Sara Davis. "An Evolving Country Begins to Accept Sara, Once David." *New York Times,* February 3, 2013.

Cacioppo, John T., and William Patrick. *Loneliness: Human Nature and the Need for Social Connection.* New York: Norton, 2008.

Cahill, Lisa Sowle, John Garvey, and T. Frank Kennedy, SJ. *Sexuality and the U.S. Catholic Church: Crisis and Renewal.* New York: Crossroad, 2006.

Callahan, Sidney. "Homosexuality, Moral Theology, and Scientific Evidence." In *Sexuality, Diversity and Catholicism: Toward the Development of Moral Theology,* ed. Patricia Jung with Joseph Corey. Collegeville, Minnesota: Liturgical Press, 2001, 201–215.

Carey, Benedict. "Psychiatric Giant Sorry for Backing Gay 'Cure.'" *New York Times,* May 18, 2012.

Carmichael, Liz. *Friendship: A Way of Interpreting Christian Love.* New York: Continuum Books, 2004.

Clendenen, Avis. "A Rare Humility and a Future-Facing Myth." *Review for Religious* 69.3 (2010): 268–280.

Coakley, Sarah. "Pleasure Principles—Toward a Contemporary Theology of Desire." *Harvard Divinity Bulletin* 33, no. 2 (autumn 2005).

Cohen, Richard, and James Marsh, eds. *Ricoeur as Another: The Ethics of Subjectivity.* New York: SUNY Press, 2002.

Cook, Ann Thompson. *Made in God's Image.* Publication of Dumbarton United Methodist Church, Washington, DC, 2003.

Cotter, Jim. "Homosexual and Holy." *The Way* (July 1988): 231–243.

Doyle, Thomas. "Canon Law and the Clergy Sex Abuse: The Failure from Above." In *Sin against Innocents: Sexual Abuse by Priests and the Role of the Catholic Church,* ed.Thomas Plante. Westport, CT: Praeger, 2004, 25–37.

Eisland, Nancy. *The Disabled God: Toward a Liberating Theology of Disability.* Nashville: Abindon Press, 1994.

Ellison, Marvin, and Kelly Brown Douglas, eds. *Sexuality and the Sacred: Sources for Theological Reflection,* 2nd ed. Louisville: Westminster John Knox, 2010.

———. "Re-imagining Good Sex: The Eroticizing of Mutual Respect and Pleasure." In *Sexuality and the Sacred,* ed Marvin Ellison and Kelly Brown Douglas. Louisville: Westminster John Knox Press, 2010, 245–261.

Epstein, Mark. *Thoughts without a Thinker.* New York: Basic Books, 1995.

———. *Open to Desire.* New York: Penguin, 2005.

Erikson, Erik. *Toys and Reasons.* New York: Norton, 1977.

———. *Identity: Youth and Crisis.* New York: Norton, 1968.

Eugenides, Jeffrey. *Middlesex.* New York: Knopf, 2002.

Farley, Margaret. *Just Love: A Framework for Christian Social Ethics.* New York: Continuum Books, 2006.

————. "Ethics, Ecclesiology and the Grace of Self-Doubt." In *A Call to Fidelity*, ed. James Walter, Timothy O'Connell, and Thomas Shannon. Washington, DC: Georgetown University Press, 2002, 55–75.

Fields, Tiffany. *Touch*. Cambridge, MA: MIT Press, 2001.

Fisher, Helen. *Why We Love: The Nature and Chemistry of Romantic Love*. New York: Holt, 2004.

Gallagher, Michael Paul. *Clashing Symbols*. New York: Paulist Press, 1998.

Garrison, Becky. "Crossing Boundaries: A Transgender Priest Becomes a University Chaplain." A report for a project of the John C. Danforth Center on Religion and Politics, Washington University in St. Louis. January 3, 2013.

Gaventa, William, and David Coulter, eds. *The Theological Voice of Wolf Wolfensberger*. Binghamton, New York: Haworth Pastoral Press, 2001.

Gregory of Nyssa. *The Life of Moses*, transl. Abraham Malherbe and Everett Ferguson. New York: Paulist Press, 1978.

————. *Commentary on the Song of Songs*, translated with an Introduction by Casimir McCambley. Brookline, Massachusetts: Hellenic College Press, 1987.

Haight, Roger. *Christian Spirituality for Seekers*. Maryknoll, New York: Orbis Books, 2012.

Hanh, Thich Nhat, and Lillian Cheung. *Savor: Mindful Eating, Mindful Life*. New York: HarperCollins, 2010.

Hemon, Alexander. "Beyond the Matrix" (on filmmaker Lana Wachowski). *New Yorker*, September 10, 2012, 66–75.

Hinze, Bradford. "Ecclesial Laments: What Can We Learn from Our Laments?" *Theological Studies* 72, no. 3(September, 2011): 470–495.

Horchow, Roger, and Sally Horchow. *The Art of Friendship*. New York: St. Martin's Press, 2006.

Howes, Hilary. "To Be or Not to Be: A Catholic Transsexual Speaks." *Conscience* XXXI, no. 2 (2010): 42–43.

Hull, John. "A Spirituality of Disability: The Christian Heritage as Both Problem and Potential." *Studies in Christian Ethics* 16, no. 2 (2003): 21–35.

Ignatieff, Michael. *The Needs of Strangers*. New York: Henry Holt, 1984.

John Paul II. *Familiaris Consortio*. In *The Post-Synodal Apostolic Exhortations of John Paul II*, ed. J. Michael Miller. Huntington, IN: Our Sunday Visitor, 1998, 148–233.

Jung, Patricia Beattie, with Joseph Coray, eds. *Sexual Diversity and Catholicism*. Collegeville, MN: Liturgical Press, 2001.

Karen, Robert. *Becoming Attached: First Relationships and How They Shape Our Capacity to Love*. New York: Oxford University Press, 1994.

Keenan, James. *Moral Wisdom*. New York: Rowman & Littlefield, 2004.

———. "The Open Debate: Moral Theology and the Lives of Gay and Lesbian Persons." *Theological Studies* 64 (2003): 127–150.

———. "Notes on Moral Theology: Living the Truth: Fundamental Theological Ethics." *Theological Studies* 73 (2012): 151–168.

Keltner, Dacher. *Born to Be Good: The Science of a Meaningful Life*. New York: Norton, 2009.

Klarman, Michael. *From the Closet to the Altar: Courts, Backlash and the Struggle for Same-Sex Marriage*. New York: Oxford University Press, 2012.

Knight, Heather. "Project Gubbio at St. Boniface: Sanctuary of Sleep." *SFGate*, March 12, 2012.

Laird, Melvin. "Under Solomon's Tutelage: The Education of Desire in the Homilies on the Song of Songs." In *Re-thinking Gregory of Nyssa*, ed. Sarah Coakley. Oxford: Blackwell, 2003, 77–95.

Lawler, Michael. "Becoming Married in the Catholic Church: A Traditional Post-Modern Proposal." *Intams Journal* 7 (spring 2001): 37–54.

Lawler, Michael, and Todd Salzman. "Virtue Ethics: Natural and Christian." *Theological Studies* 74 (2013): 442–473.

Lebacqz, Karen. "Appropriate Vulnerability: A Sexual Ethic for Singles." In *Sexuality: A Reader*, ed. Karen Lebacqz and David Sinacore-Guinn. NewYork: Pilgrim Press, 2001.

Lewis, Thomas, Fari Amini, and Richard Lannon. *A General Theory of Love*. New York: Vintage, 2001.

Lovett, Ian. "After 37 Years of Trying to Change People's Sexual Orientation, Group to Disband." *New York Times*, June 21, 2013.

MacIntyre, Alasdair. *Dependent Rational Animals: Why Human Beings Need the Virtues*. Chicago: Open Court, 1999.

Mahoney, John. *The Making of Moral Theology*. New York: Oxford University Press, 1987.

McFague, Sallie. *Transcendence and Beyond*, ed. John Caputo and Michael Scanlon. Bloomington, IN: Indiana University Press, 2007, 151–168.

McGinnis, Alan Loy. *The Friendship Factor*. Updated edition. Minneapolis, MN: Augsburg Press, 2010.

Markham, Donna, and Samuel Mikail. "Perpetrators of Clergy Abuse of Minors: Insights from Attachment Theory." In *Sin against Innocents:*

Sexual Abuse by Priests and the Role of the Catholic Church, ed. Thomas Plante. Westport, CT: Praeger, 2004, 101–114.

Marriage: Love and Life in the Divine Plan. A Pastoral Letter of the United States Conference of Catholic Bishops (2009). Available at http://www.usccb.org.

Miles, Margaret. *Desire and Delight: A New Reading of Augustine's Confessions.* New York: Crossroad, 1992.

Miller, Vassar. *If I Had Wheels or Love: The Collected Poems of Vassar Miller.* Dallas, TX: Southern Methodist University Press, 1991.

Moore, Gareth. "Christians and Same-Sex Unions." *Intams Review* 7 (2001): 95–97.

Morris, Jan. *Conundrum.* New York: Harcourt Brace Jovanovich, 1974.

Muldoon, Tim. *The Ignatian Workout: Daily Spiritual Exercises for a Healthy Faith.* Chicago: Loyola University Press, 2004, 33–35.

Neiman, Susan. *Moral Clarity.* New York: Harcourt, 2008.

Nelson, Shasta. *Friendships Don't Just Happen.* Kindle edition.

Nussbaum, Martha. *Upheavals of Thought: The Intelligence of Emotions.* New York: Cambridge University Press, 2001.

———. *Hiding from Humanity: Disgust, Shame, and the Law.* Princeton, NJ: Princeton University Press, 2004.

———. *The Fragility of Goodness, Luck and Ethics in Greek Tragedy and Philosophy.* New York: Cambridge University Press, 2001 [revised edition])

———. *Frontiers of Justice.* Cambridge, MA: Harvard University Press, 2006.

O'Donnell, James. *Augustine, A New Biography.* New York: Harper, 2005.

Oppenheimer, Mark. "In Shift, an Activist Enlists Same-Sex Couples in a Pro-Marriage Coalition." *New York Times,* January 30, 2013.

Paul, Marla. *The Friendship Crisis: Finding, Making, and Keeping Friends.* New York: St. Martin's Press, 2004.

Perez-Pena, Richard. "College Health Plans Respond as Transgender Students Gain Visibility." *The New York Times,* February 12, 2012.

PFLAG (Parents and Friends of Lesbians and Gays). Welcoming Our Trans Family and Friends, available at www.pflag.org.

Philibert, Paul. "Readiness for Ritual: Psychological Aspects of Maturity in Christian Celebration." In *Alternative Futures for Worship, Vol. 1: General Introduction,* ed. Regis Duffy, Michael Cowan, Paul Philibert, and Edward Kilmartin. Collegeville, MN: Liturgical Press, 1987, 63–212.

Plutarch. *On Love, the Family, and the Good Life, Selected Essays of Plutarch,* translated by Moses Hadas. New York: Mentor Books, 1957.

Pope, Stephen. "The Magisterium's Arguments against 'Same-Sex Marriage': An Ethical Analysis and Critique." *Theological Studies* 65 (2004): 530–565.

Ricoeur, Paul. "Wonder, Eroticism, and Enigma." In *Sexuality and the Sacred: Sources for Theological Reflection,* ed. James Nelson and Sandra Longfellow. Louisville, KY: Westminster/John Knox, 1994, 8–84.

———. *Figuring the Sacred.* Minneapolis, MN: Fortress Press, 1995.

Robinson, Geoffrey. *Confronting Power and Sex in the Catholic Church.* Collegeville, MN: Liturgical Press, 2008.

Rossetti, Steven. *A Tragic Grace: The Catholic Church and Child Sexual Abuse.* Collegeville, MN: Liturgical Press, 1996.

Rubio, Julie Hanlon. *Family Ethics: Practices for Christians.* Washington, DC: Georgetown University Press, 2010.

Salzman, Todd, Thomas Kelly, and John O'Keefe, eds. *Marriage in the Catholic Tradition: Scripture, Tradition, and Experience.* New York: Crossroad, 2004.

Sandal, Michael. *Justice: What's the Right Thing to Do?* New York: Farrar, Straus and Giroux, 2009.

Scarry, Elaine. *On Beauty and Being Just.* Princeton, NJ: Princeton University Press, 1999.

Seelye, Katherine. "Private Pain, Played Out on Public Stage." *New York Times,* January 14, 2013.

Sheehy, Sandy. *Connecting: The Enduring Power of Female Friendship.* New York: Wm. Morrow, 2000.

Siegel, Daniel. *Mindsight.* New York: Bantam Books, 2010.

———. *The Developing Mind: How Relationships and the Brain Interact to Shape Who We Are.* New York: Guilford Press, 1999.

Smith, J. Warren. *Passion and Paradise: Human and Divine Emotion in the Thought of Gregory of Nyssa.* New York: Crossroad, 2004.

Solomon, Andrew. *Far from the Tree. Parents, Children, and the Search for Identity.* New York: Scribner, 2012.

Spohn, William. "The Reasoning Heart: An American Approach to Christian Discernment." *Theological Studies* 44 (1983): 30–52.

———. "Jesus and Christian Ethics." *Theological Studies* 56 (1995): 92–107.

————. "Episcopal Responsibility for the Sexual Abuse Crisis." In *Sin against Innocents: Sexual Abuse by Priests and the Role of the Catholic Church,* (ed.) Thomas Plante. Westport, CT: Praeger, 2004, 155–167.

Stalnaker, Aaron. *Overcoming Our Evil: Human Nature and Spiritual Exercises in Xunzi and Augustine.* Washington, DC: Georgetown University Press, 2006.

Stewart, James B. "Refusing to be Late on Gay Marriage." *New York Times,* March 2, 2013.

Stuart, Elizabeth. "Disruptive Bodies: Disability, Embodiment and Sexuality." In *Sexuality and the Sacred: Sources of Theological Reflection,* ed. Marvin Ellison and Kelly Brown Douglas. Louisville, KY: Westminster John Knox Press, 2010, 322–337.

Sullivan, Andrew. *Virtually Normal.* New York: Knopf, 1996.

Swenson, Erin. "Pastoral Care in Transgender Experience." The Southern Association for Gender Education [SAGE], Institute for Welcoming Resources, 2001.

Tanis, Justin. *Transgender: Theology, Ministry and Communities of Faith.* Cleveland, OH: Pilgrim Press, 2003.

Taylor, Charles. "Iris Murdoch and Moral Philosophy." in *Dilemmas and Connections.* Cambridge, MA: Harvard University Press, 2011, 3–23.

————. "A Catholic Modernity?" In *Dilemmas and Connections.* Cambridge, MA: Harvard University Press, 2011, 45–79.

Tracy, David. *Plurality and Ambiguity.* San Francisco: Harper and Row, 1987.

Traina, Christina. *Erotic Attunement: Parenthood and the Ethics of Sensuality between Unequals.* Chicago: University of Chicago Press, 2011.

———. "Papal Ideals, Marital Realities: One View from the Ground." In *Sexual Diversity and Catholicism: Toward the Development of Moral Theology*, ed. Patricia Beattie Jung, with Joseph Andrew Coray. Collegeville, MN: The Liturgical Press, 2001, 269–288.

———. "Under Pressure: Sexual Discipleship in the Real World." In *Sexuality and the U.S. Catholic Church,* ed. Lisa Sowle Cahill, John Garvey, and Frank Kennedy. New York: Crossroad, 2006, 68–93.

———. "Roman Catholic Resources for an Ethic of Sexuality." Paper delivered at the Common Ground Conference, March 5–7, 2004.

TRANS. DVD, available at www.Transthemovie.com.

Unger, Roberto. *The Self Awakened.* Cambridge, MA: Harvard University Press, 2007.

Way, Nicole. *Boys' Friendships and the Crisis of Connection*. Cambridge, MA: Harvard University Press, 2011.

Whitehead, James D., and Evelyn Eaton Whitehead. *Holy Eros: Recovering the Passion of God.* Maryknoll, NY: Orbis Books, 2009.

———. "Transgender Lives: From Bewilderment to God's Extravagance." *Pastoral Psychology* 63 (2014): 171--184. doi: 10.1007/s11089-013-0543-7.

———. Born in Grace: Gender-Diverse Children. See www.FortunateFamilies.com.

———. "International Transgender Day of Remembrance. *National Catholic Reporter* (www.ncronline.org), November 19, 2012.

———. "An Epiphany of Transgender Lives." *National Catholic Reporter,* January 4, 2013.

Williams, Mark, John Teasdale, Zindel Segal, Jon Kabat-Zinn, eds. *The Mindful Way through Depression*. London: Guilford Press, 2007.

Wright, Wendy. "Marriage as a 'School of Love'." Paper delivered at the Promoting and Sustaining Marriage as a Community of Life and Love Colloquium, October 24–25, 2005.

Yearley, Lee. "Ethics of Bewilderment." *Journal of Religious Ethics* 38 (2010): 436–460.

Index

overextension, as frequent characterization of lifestyle of marriages, 41

P

panis angelicus (bread of angels), 4
"Papal Ideals, Marital Realities: One View from the Ground" (Traina), 101
parenthood/parenting
   lesson of fruitfulness, 97
   marriage and, 40–41
Parton, Dolly, 134
Partridge, Cameron, 169, 177
Passion and Paradise: Human and Divine Emotion in the Thought of Gregory of Nyssa (Smith), 113
pastoral care, for members of trans community, 174–175
"Pastoral Care in Transgender Experience" (Swenson), 177
Paul (biblical), 77, 82, 94
Paul (saint), 111, 147, 163–164
Paula, Marla, 34
Pepper, Rachel, 149, 157, 160, 164
Perl, Fritz, 120
permanence, as commitment of marriage, 39
"Perpetrators of Clergy Abuse of Minors: Insights from Attachment Theory" (Markham and Mikail), 91
personal resources, commitment to development of, 51
Perspectives on Marriage (Scott and Warren, eds.), 45
phobias, 125–126
physical ambiguities, 161
physical embodiment, 134
physical gender, 155
physical infirmity, spiritual integrity as linked to/dependent upon, 77
physical touch, as first language, 5

physical well-being, becoming more intentional about, 50
physiological arousal, 33
Pius XI (pope), 96
Plante, Thomas, 90
pleasure, according to Augustine, 109
Pleasure, Pain and Passion (Cotter), 13
"Pleasure Principles—Toward a Contemporary Theology of Desire" (Coakley), 113
Plutarch, 94–95, 101
Pope, Stephen, 100, 101, 102, 127, 128
Pope Benedict XVI, 70
Pope Francis, 90
Pope John Paul II, 96, 98
Pope Pius XI, 96, 102
Porter, Jean, 100
practices, as purposeful actions, 47
prejudice, 18, 19, 126–127, 147, 170, 173, 174, 177
priests, as symbolic persons, 86–87, 88
Prince, 134
"Private Pain, Played Out on Public Stage" (Seelve), 91
procreation, 94, 97–98, 99, 100, 106, 176
"Project Gubbio at St. Boniface: Sanctuary of Sleep" (Knight), 71
prophetic imagination, 179–187
The Prophetic Imagination (Brueggemann), 180, 187
Protestant Reformation, 4
Psalm
   34:8, 11
   82, 173
   139:13, 151
pseudo-intimacy, 44

R

Rankin, Susan, 149, 164, 168, 177
rape
   of the soul, 160
   as strategy of war, 62
"A Rare Humility and a Future-Facing Myth" (Clendenen), 149

TRUE DIRECTIONS
An affiliate of Tarcher Books

OUR MISSION

Tarcher's mission has always been to publish books
that contain great ideas. Why? Because:

GREAT LIVES BEGIN WITH GREAT IDEAS

At Tarcher, we recognize that many talented authors, speakers, educators,
and thought-leaders share this mission and deserve to be published—
many more than Tarcher can reasonably publish ourselves. True
Directions is ideal for authors and books that increase awareness, raise
consciousness, and inspire others to live their ideals and passions.

Like Tarcher, True Directions books are designed to do three things:
inspire, inform, and motivate.

Thus, True Directions is an ideal way for these important voices to
bring their messages of hope, healing, and help to the world.

Every book published by True Directions—whether it is non-fiction, memoir,
novel, poetry or children's book—continues Tarcher's mission to publish works
that bring positive change in the world. We invite you to join our mission.

For more information, see the True Directions website:
www.iUniverse.com/TrueDirections/SignUp

Be a part of Tarcher's community to bring positive change in this world!
See exclusive author videos, discover new and exciting books, learn about
upcoming events, connect with author blogs and websites, and more!
www.tarcherbooks.com

TRUE DIRECTIONS
AN AFFILIATE OF TARCHER BOOKS